FRANKFURT Travel Guide

Welcome to Frankfurt, a vibrant and dynamic city located in the heart of Germany. With its rich history, stunning architecture, and thriving cultural scene, Frankfurt is a destination that has something to offer everyone, whether you're a history buff, foodie, art lover, or just looking for a fun and memorable vacation.

In this travel guide, we'll take you on a journey through the best that Frankfurt has to offer, from its iconic landmarks and must-see attractions to its hidden gems and off-the-beaten-path destinations. You'll discover the city's fascinating history, explore its stunning natural beauty, and indulge in its world-renowned culinary scene.

Whether you're visiting Frankfurt for the first time or returning for another adventure, this guide has everything you need to make the most of your trip. So sit back, relax, and get ready to discover all that this amazing city has to offer!

Contents

I. Introduction

About Frankfurt

Frankfurt is a bustling metropolis located in the heart of Germany. It is the fifth-largest city in the country, and a hub for commerce, culture, and tourism. This vibrant city offers visitors an exciting mix of history, modernity, and cultural diversity, making it an ideal destination for travelers seeking an authentic German experience.

Frankfurt has a rich history, dating back over 2,000 years. It played a pivotal role in the Holy Roman Empire and was also the birthplace of Germany's most famous writer, Johann Wolfgang von Goethe. The city was heavily bombed during World War II, but has since undergone significant reconstruction to become the modern and thriving city it is today.

Frankfurt is known for its impressive skyline, which is dominated by towering skyscrapers and modern architecture. The city is also home to a wide range of museums, galleries, and cultural institutions, showcasing everything from classical art to contemporary design.

Frankfurt is a city of contrasts, where traditional German culture meets modern cosmopolitanism. It is a city that is proud of its past, but also embraces the future with open arms. Whether you're interested in history, culture, shopping, or cuisine, Frankfurt is sure to have something to offer every type of traveler.

Why Visit Frankfurt?

There are countless reasons why Frankfurt should be on your travel bucket list. Here are just a few:

1. Rich History: Frankfurt has a fascinating past, dating back over two millennia. From its role in the Holy Roman Empire to its more recent history as a center of finance and commerce, there

is no shortage of historical landmarks and cultural institutions to explore.

2. Cultural Diversity: Frankfurt is a melting pot of cultures and nationalities, with a thriving arts scene and a range of cultural events and festivals throughout the year. Whether you're interested in classical music, modern art, or international cuisine, Frankfurt has something to offer.

3. Modern Architecture: The city's skyline is dominated by towering skyscrapers and contemporary architecture, making it a mecca for fans of modern design and urban landscapes.

4. Shopping: Frankfurt is a shopper's paradise, with everything from luxury boutiques to traditional markets offering a wide range of goods and souvenirs.

5. Convenient Location: Frankfurt is centrally located in Europe, making it a great starting point for exploring other parts of Germany and beyond. It is also home to one of Europe's busiest airports, making it easy to access from anywhere in the world.

6. Nightlife: Frankfurt has a vibrant nightlife scene, with everything from traditional beer halls to trendy clubs and bars.

Whether you're interested in history, culture, or simply soaking up the atmosphere of a bustling European city, Frankfurt has something to offer every type of traveler. With its rich history, cultural diversity, and modern amenities, it's easy to see why Frankfurt is a must-visit destination.

Getting to Frankfurt

Frankfurt is a major transportation hub, with excellent connections by air, rail, and road. Here are some of the best ways to get to Frankfurt:

By Air:

Frankfurt is home to one of Europe's busiest airports, Frankfurt Airport (FRA), which is located just 12 km (7.5 miles) southwest of the city center. The airport serves as a hub for several major airlines, including Lufthansa, and offers direct flights to destinations all over the world. From the airport, you can take a taxi, train, or bus to reach the city center.

By Train:

Frankfurt has excellent rail connections, with several high-speed trains (ICE) and regional trains serving the city. Frankfurt's main train station, Frankfurt Hauptbahnhof, is located in the city center and offers connections to cities throughout Germany and Europe.

By Car:

Frankfurt is well-connected to Germany's extensive highway network, with several major highways (Autobahns) passing through the city. However, driving in the city center can be challenging, and parking can be expensive. If you do decide to drive, it's best to park outside of the city center and use public transportation to reach your destination.

By Bus:

Several bus companies operate services to Frankfurt from other major cities in Germany and Europe. The main bus station in Frankfurt is located next to the train station, making it easy to connect to other modes of transportation.

Once you arrive in Frankfurt, getting around the city is easy thanks to its excellent public transportation system, which includes buses, trams, and an extensive subway network (U-Bahn). Taxis and rental bikes are also readily available.

II. Top Tourist Attractions in Frankfurt

The Römerberg

The Römerberg is the historic heart of Frankfurt and one of the city's most popular tourist destinations. Located in the Altstadt (Old Town), the Römerberg is home to several historic buildings, including the Römer, Frankfurt's city hall, and the Alte Nikolaikirche, a medieval church.

The Römerberg dates back to the 12th century and has served as a market square and meeting place for centuries. Today, it is a pedestrian zone and a hub of activity, with a range of cafes, restaurants, and shops lining its cobblestone streets.

One of the highlights of the Römerberg is the Römer, which has served as Frankfurt's city hall for over 600 years. The building's iconic facade features a series of gabled roofs and a statue of Justice at the top. The Römer has been the site of many important events throughout Frankfurt's history, including coronations and treaty signings.

Another notable building on the Römerberg is the Alte Nikolaikirche, a Gothic church that dates back to the 13th century. The church was heavily damaged during World War II but has since been restored and now serves as a venue for concerts and cultural events.

Visitors to the Römerberg can also enjoy a range of outdoor cafes, street performers, and market stalls selling local crafts and souvenirs. The square is particularly picturesque at night when it is lit up by street lamps and the colorful facades of the surrounding buildings.

Visitor Information:

- Location: Römerberg, 60311 Frankfurt am Main, Germany

- Getting there: The Römerberg is located in the Altstadt and can be easily reached on foot or by public transportation. The nearest U-Bahn station is Römerberg, which is served by the U4 subway line.

Goethe House and Museum

The Goethe House and Museum is a must-visit destination for literature and history enthusiasts. The house is the birthplace and childhood home of Johann Wolfgang von Goethe, one of Germany's most famous writers and poets.

Located in the heart of Frankfurt's Altstadt (Old Town), the Goethe House is a well-preserved 18th-century building that offers visitors a glimpse into the life and times of Goethe and his family. The museum houses a vast collection of original artifacts, including furniture, artwork, and personal belongings that belonged to the Goethe family.

The museum is divided into several rooms, each showcasing a different aspect of Goethe's life and work. Highlights include the study, where Goethe wrote many of his famous works, and the garden, which features a bust of the writer and a variety of plants and flowers that would have been common in the 18th century.

One of the most interesting exhibits in the museum is the collection of Goethe's original manuscripts and letters, which offer a unique insight into his creative process and personal life. Visitors can also view several portraits of Goethe and his family, as well as a range of other artworks from the 18th and 19th centuries.

Visitor Information:

- Location: Großer Hirschgraben 23-25, 60311 Frankfurt am Main, Germany

- Hours: Tuesday-Sunday: 10am-6pm, Closed on Mondays

- Admission: Adults: €7, Concessions: €3.50, Children under 12: Free

- Getting there: The Goethe House and Museum is located in the Altstadt and can be easily reached on foot or by public transportation. The nearest U-Bahn station is Dom/Römer, which is served by the U4 and U5 subway lines.

Some of the most interesting exhibits at the Goethe House and Museum include:

- Goethe's original manuscripts and letters

- Furniture and artwork from the 18th and 19th centuries

- Portraits of Goethe and his family

- The study where Goethe wrote many of his famous works

- The garden, featuring a bust of the writer and plants from the 18th century

St. Paul's Church

St. Paul's Church, also known as Paulskirche, is a historic church located in the heart of Frankfurt. The church has a significant place in German history as it was the site of the first democratically elected parliament in Germany in 1848.

The church was built between 1789 and 1833 and is a fine example of classical architecture. It was heavily damaged during World War II but has since been restored to its former glory. Today, the church serves as a venue for cultural events and exhibitions, as well as a memorial to the struggle for democracy in Germany.

Visitors to St. Paul's Church can admire the impressive neoclassical facade and the spacious interior, which features a central dome and a range of decorative elements, including frescoes and statues.

The church also houses a range of historical artifacts and exhibits related to its role in German history.

One of the highlights of a visit to St. Paul's Church is the panoramic view of Frankfurt from the roof terrace. Visitors can climb to the top of the church's tower for an unforgettable view of the city skyline.

Visitor Information:

- Location: Paulsplatz 11, 60311 Frankfurt am Main, Germany

- Hours: Monday-Saturday: 10am-5pm, Sunday: 11am-5pm

- Admission: Free

- Getting there: St. Paul's Church is located in the Altstadt and can be easily reached on foot or by public transportation. The nearest U-Bahn station is Dom/Römer, which is served by the U4 and U5 subway lines.

Some of the most interesting features and exhibits at St. Paul's Church include:

- The neoclassical facade and spacious interior

- Historical artifacts and exhibits related to German history

- Panoramic views of Frankfurt from the roof terrace

- The church's role in the struggle for democracy in Germany.

Frankfurt Cathedral

Frankfurt Cathedral, also known as Frankfurter Dom, is a stunning Gothic church located in the heart of Frankfurt's Altstadt (Old Town). The cathedral is one of the city's most iconic landmarks and a popular destination for tourists and locals alike.

The cathedral was originally built in the 14th century and has undergone several renovations and restorations over the centuries. The building's impressive facade features a series of intricate stone carvings and stained glass windows, while the interior is decorated with beautiful frescoes, sculptures, and religious artwork.

Visitors to Frankfurt Cathedral can explore the interior of the church, which features a range of historical artifacts and exhibits related to its long and fascinating history. Highlights include the ornate high altar, the beautiful stained glass windows, and the impressive organ, which dates back to the 18th century.

One of the most popular features of Frankfurt Cathedral is its tower, which offers stunning panoramic views of the city. Visitors can climb to the top of the tower for an unforgettable view of

Frankfurt's skyline, including the nearby Römerberg and Main River.

Visitor Information:

- Location: Domplatz 1, 60311 Frankfurt am Main, Germany

- Hours: Monday-Saturday: 9am-7pm, Sunday: 1pm-7pm

- Admission: Free, but donations are appreciated

- Tower Admission: Adults: €5, Concessions: €3, Children under 6: Free

- Getting there: Frankfurt Cathedral is located in the Altstadt and can be easily reached on foot or by public transportation. The nearest U-Bahn station is Dom/Römer, which is served by the U4 and U5 subway lines.

Some of the most interesting features and exhibits at Frankfurt Cathedral include:

- The ornate high altar

- The beautiful stained glass windows

- The impressive organ, which dates back to the 18th century

- The tower, which offers stunning panoramic views of the city

Palmengarten

Palmengarten is a beautiful botanical garden located in the Westend district of Frankfurt. The garden covers an area of 22 hectares (54 acres) and features a stunning collection of plants from all over the world.

The garden was established in 1868 and has since grown to become one of the most popular attractions in Frankfurt. Visitors to

Palmengarten can explore a range of different themed gardens, including a Japanese garden, a rose garden, and a tropical greenhouse.

One of the highlights of Palmengarten is the impressive Palm House, a large greenhouse that is home to a variety of exotic plants and tropical flowers. The greenhouse was built in the early 20th century and features a stunning glass and steel design.

Visitors to Palmengarten can also enjoy a range of seasonal events and exhibitions, including live music performances, art exhibitions, and guided tours of the gardens.

Visitor Information:

- Location: Siesmayerstraße 61, 60323 Frankfurt am Main, Germany

- Hours: Daily: 9am-6pm (closing time varies depending on the season)

- Admission: Adults: €7, Concessions: €2.50-€4, Children under 6: Free

- Getting there: Palmengarten is located in the Westend district and can be easily reached by public transportation. The nearest U-Bahn station is Bockenheimer Warte, which is served by the U4 and U6 subway lines.

Some of the most interesting features and exhibits at Palmengarten include:

- The Palm House, with its stunning glass and steel design

- The Japanese garden, featuring a traditional tea house and stone lanterns

- The rose garden, which boasts over 2,000 different types of roses

- The tropical greenhouse, home to a variety of exotic plants and flowers from around the world.

Main Tower

Main Tower is a modern skyscraper located in the heart of Frankfurt's financial district. The tower stands at a height of 200 meters (656 feet) and is one of the tallest buildings in the city.

The tower was completed in 1999 and is home to a range of businesses and offices. However, it is also a popular tourist attraction, thanks to its observation deck, which offers stunning panoramic views of Frankfurt and the surrounding area.

Visitors to Main Tower can take a high-speed elevator to the observation deck, which is located on the 56th floor. From there, they can enjoy unobstructed views of Frankfurt's skyline, including the nearby Römerberg and the Main River. On clear days, it is possible to see as far as the Taunus Mountains.

Main Tower also features a restaurant and bar on the 53rd floor, where visitors can enjoy a range of international cuisine and cocktails while taking in the breathtaking views.

Visitor Information:

- Location: Neue Mainzer Str. 52-58, 60311 Frankfurt am Main, Germany

- Hours: Monday-Saturday: 10am-9pm, Sunday and Holidays: 11am-7pm

- Admission: Adults: €7.50, Concessions: €5, Children under 7: Free

- Getting there: Main Tower is located in the financial district and can be easily reached by public transportation. The nearest U-

Bahn station is Willy-Brandt-Platz, which is served by the U1, U2, U3, and U8 subway lines.

Some of the most interesting features and exhibits at Main Tower include:

- The observation deck, offering stunning panoramic views of Frankfurt

- The high-speed elevator, which travels to the 56th floor in just seconds

- The restaurant and bar, offering international cuisine and cocktails with a view of the city.

Senckenberg Natural History Museum

The Senckenberg Natural History Museum is one of the largest natural history museums in Europe and a must-visit destination for anyone interested in the natural world. The museum is located in Frankfurt's Bockenheim district and is home to an extensive collection of fossils, minerals, and specimens from all over the world.

The museum was founded in 1817 and has since grown to become one of the most important scientific institutions in Germany. The museum's collection includes over 40 million specimens, making it one of the largest natural history collections in the world.

Visitors to the Senckenberg Natural History Museum can explore a range of different exhibits, covering everything from dinosaurs to the evolution of humans. Highlights include a life-size replica of a T-Rex, a collection of rare gemstones and minerals, and a range of exhibits on climate change and sustainability.

One of the most popular exhibits at the museum is the Biodiversity Wall, a stunning display that showcases the incredible diversity of life on Earth. The wall features over 1,500 mounted specimens, including mammals, birds, reptiles, and insects, arranged according to their taxonomic order.

Visitor Information:

- Location: Senckenberganlage 25, 60325 Frankfurt am Main, Germany

- Hours: Daily: 9am-5pm (closed on Mondays from October to March)

- Admission: Adults: €9, Concessions: €6, Children under 6: Free

- Getting there: The Senckenberg Natural History Museum is located in the Bockenheim district and can be easily reached by public transportation. The nearest U-Bahn station is Bockenheimer Warte, which is served by the U4 and U6 subway lines.

Some of the most interesting exhibits at the Senckenberg Natural History Museum include:

- The life-size T-Rex replica

- The Biodiversity Wall, showcasing the diversity of life on Earth

- The collection of rare gemstones and minerals

- Exhibits on climate change and sustainability

- Collections of fossils, specimens, and taxidermy animals from all over the world.

III. Hidden Gems in Frankfurt

Kleinmarkthalle

Kleinmarkthalle is a bustling indoor market located in the heart of Frankfurt's city center. The market has been in operation since 1879 and is a popular destination for foodies and locals alike.

The market features over 60 vendors, offering a wide range of fresh produce, meats, cheeses, and baked goods. Visitors to Kleinmarkthalle can shop for everything from exotic fruits and vegetables to local meats and sausages.

One of the highlights of Kleinmarkthalle is the seafood section, which features a variety of fresh fish and shellfish from the North Sea and Baltic Sea. Visitors can also sample a range of international foods, including Italian pasta, French cheese, and Middle Eastern spices.

In addition to the food vendors, Kleinmarkthalle also features several cafes and restaurants, where visitors can sit and enjoy a cup of coffee or a delicious meal. The market's vibrant atmosphere and friendly vendors make it a great place to experience the local culture and cuisine.

Visitor Information:

- Location: Hasengasse 5-7, 60311 Frankfurt am Main, Germany

- Hours: Monday-Friday: 8am-6pm, Saturday: 8am-4pm

- Admission: Free

- Getting there: Kleinmarkthalle is located in the city center and can be easily reached on foot or by public transportation. The nearest U-Bahn station is Hauptwache, which is served by the U1, U2, U3, U6, and U7 subway lines.

Some of the most popular vendors at Kleinmarkthalle include:

- Schreiber's Fine Wines and Spirits, offering a range of local and international wines and spirits

- Metzgerei Schreiber, a local butcher selling a variety of meats and sausages

- Fisch Witte, offering fresh seafood from the North Sea and Baltic Sea

- Bäckerei Wegerich, a bakery selling freshly baked bread and pastries

- Delikatessenhalle, a gourmet food stall selling a range of international foods and delicacies.

Old Sachsenhausen

Old Sachsenhausen is a charming neighborhood located on the south bank of the Main River in Frankfurt. The area is known for its traditional half-timbered houses, narrow streets, and lively nightlife.

The neighborhood has a long history, dating back to the 12th century, and has remained a popular destination for locals and visitors alike. Visitors to Old Sachsenhausen can stroll along the cobbled streets, stopping at one of the many traditional taverns and bars that line the neighborhood's narrow alleys.

One of the highlights of Old Sachsenhausen is the Apfelwein (apple wine) culture. The neighborhood is home to several traditional apple wine taverns, where visitors can sample the local specialty, served in traditional blue and white pottery pitchers.

In addition to the taverns and bars, Old Sachsenhausen is also home to a range of shops, restaurants, and cafes. Visitors can shop for souvenirs and gifts, dine on local cuisine, or simply enjoy a cup of coffee while soaking up the neighborhood's charming atmosphere.

Visitor Information:

- Location: Sachsenhausen, 60594 Frankfurt am Main, Germany

- Hours: Most restaurants and bars open in the late afternoon and evening

- Admission: Free

- Getting there: Old Sachsenhausen is located on the south bank of the Main River and can be easily reached on foot or by public transportation. The nearest S-Bahn station is Lokalbahnhof, which is served by the S3, S4, S5, and S6 lines.

Some of the most popular attractions and activities in Old Sachsenhausen include:

- Sampling the local Apfelwein at one of the neighborhood's traditional taverns

- Strolling along the cobbled streets and admiring the half-timbered houses

- Shopping for souvenirs and gifts at the neighborhood's shops and boutiques

- Dining on local cuisine at one of the many restaurants and cafes

- Enjoying the lively nightlife and entertainment in the neighborhood.

Museum of Modern Art

The Museum of Modern Art (Museum für Moderne Kunst) is a contemporary art museum located in Frankfurt's city center. The museum's collection includes over 5,000 works of art, ranging from paintings and sculptures to installations and multimedia exhibits.

The museum was founded in 1981 and has since become one of the most important cultural institutions in Frankfurt. Visitors to the Museum of Modern Art can explore a range of different exhibits, featuring works by some of the most famous artists of the 20th and 21st centuries.

The museum's collection includes works by artists such as Francis Bacon, Gerhard Richter, and Andy Warhol, as well as a range of contemporary artists from around the world. The museum also hosts temporary exhibits and special events throughout the year.

One of the highlights of the Museum of Modern Art is its architecture. The museum's distinctive glass and steel design was created by the Austrian architect Hans Hollein and has won numerous awards for its innovative and striking appearance.

Visitor Information:

- Location: Domstraße 10, 60311 Frankfurt am Main, Germany

- Hours: Tuesday, Thursday-Sunday: 10am-6pm, Wednesday: 10am-8pm, Closed on Mondays

- Admission: Adults: €12, Concessions: €8, Children under 12: Free

- Getting there: The Museum of Modern Art is located in the city center and can be easily reached on foot or by public transportation. The nearest U-Bahn station is Dom/Römer, which is served by the U4 and U5 subway lines.

Some of the most interesting exhibits and features at the Museum of Modern Art include:

- Works by famous artists such as Francis Bacon, Gerhard Richter, and Andy Warhol

- Contemporary works by artists from around the world

- Temporary exhibits and special events throughout the year

- The museum's distinctive glass and steel architecture

- Educational programs and guided tours for visitors of all ages.

Berger Street

Berger Street (Berger Straße) is a vibrant and eclectic neighborhood located in the northern part of Frankfurt. The neighborhood is known for its lively atmosphere, trendy cafes, and quirky shops and boutiques.

The neighborhood has a rich history, dating back to the 14th century, and has since become a popular destination for locals and visitors alike. Visitors to Berger Street can stroll along the bustling thoroughfare, taking in the sights and sounds of the neighborhood's unique and colorful vibe.

One of the highlights of Berger Street is its diverse and international cuisine. The neighborhood is home to a range of restaurants and cafes, serving everything from traditional German cuisine to exotic dishes from around the world.

In addition to the food and drink, Berger Street is also known for its shopping. The neighborhood is home to a range of independent boutiques, vintage shops, and specialty stores, selling everything from handmade jewelry to second-hand records.

Visitor Information:

- Location: Berger Straße, 60316 Frankfurt am Main, Germany

- Hours: Most shops and restaurants are open throughout the day and into the evening

- Admission: Free

- Getting there: Berger Street is located in the northern part of Frankfurt and can be easily reached by public transportation. The nearest U-Bahn station is Merianplatz, which is served by the U4 subway line.

Some of the most popular attractions and activities on Berger Street include:

- Sampling the diverse and international cuisine at the neighborhood's restaurants and cafes

- Shopping for unique and quirky items at the independent boutiques and specialty stores

- Admiring the historic architecture and colorful street art

- Enjoying the neighborhood's lively atmosphere and street performers

- Exploring the nearby Bethmann Park, a beautiful green space with walking trails and a pond.

IV. Food and Drink in Frankfurt

Traditional Frankfurt Cuisine

Frankfurt is known for its hearty and flavorful cuisine, which draws on the city's rich culinary history and traditions. Many of the city's most famous dishes are made with locally sourced ingredients and feature a range of savory flavors and textures.

One of the most famous dishes in Frankfurt is the Frankfurter Würstchen, a type of small, smoked sausage that is often served with sauerkraut or potato salad. Another popular dish is the Grüne Soße, or "green sauce," which is made with seven different herbs and served cold with boiled eggs and potatoes.

Another must-try dish in Frankfurt is the *Handkäse mit Musik*, which is a type of sour milk cheese served with onions and a vinegar and oil dressing. The dish is often enjoyed with a glass of local apple wine, known as *Apfelwein.*

Other traditional Frankfurt dishes include the *Rippchen mit Kraut,* which is a dish of cured pork ribs and sauerkraut, and the Bethmännchen, which is a small, marzipan-based cookie that is traditionally served during the holiday season.

In addition to these traditional dishes, Frankfurt is also known for its wide range of international cuisine, including Italian, Turkish, and Middle Eastern food. Visitors to the city can sample a range of different flavors and cuisines, making it a great destination for foodies and adventurous eaters.

Some of the best places to try traditional Frankfurt cuisine include the local apple wine taverns, which serve a range of regional specialties, and the city's many outdoor markets and food festivals, which offer a wide range of local and international dishes.

Overall, Frankfurt's cuisine is a rich and flavorful reflection of the city's history and traditions, and is a must-try for anyone visiting the city.

Local Food Markets

Frankfurt is home to a variety of food markets, offering a wide range of fresh and locally sourced produce, meats, and baked goods. These markets are a great place to experience the local culture and cuisine, and to sample some of the city's most famous dishes.

One of the most popular markets in Frankfurt is the Kleinmarkthalle, which is a bustling indoor market located in the city center. The market features over 60 vendors, offering a range of fresh produce, meats, cheeses, and baked goods. Visitors can shop for everything from exotic fruits and vegetables to local meats and sausages, and can sample a range of international foods, including Italian pasta, French cheese, and Middle Eastern spices.

Another popular market in Frankfurt is the weekly farmers' market, held on Saturdays at the Konstablerwache. The market features a range of local and organic produce, including fruits and vegetables, meats, cheeses, and baked goods. Visitors can shop for fresh, seasonal ingredients and enjoy the lively atmosphere of the market.

For a more upscale food shopping experience, visitors can head to the Wochenmarkt Schillerstraße, a high-end market located in the city's Westend district. The market features a range of specialty food vendors, selling everything from artisanal cheeses to handmade chocolates. Visitors can also enjoy a glass of wine or a cup of coffee while browsing the market's offerings.

Overall, Frankfurt's food markets are a great way to experience the local cuisine and culture, and to shop for fresh and locally sourced ingredients. Visitors to the city should be sure to visit at least one of these markets during their stay to get a true taste of Frankfurt.

Best Restaurants and Cafes

Frankfurt is a city with a diverse culinary scene, offering a wide range of dining options for visitors. From traditional German cuisine to international flavors, the city's restaurants and cafes have something to offer for everyone. Here are some of the best places to eat in Frankfurt:

1. Apfelwein Wagner

This traditional apple wine tavern is a must-visit for anyone looking to experience Frankfurt's local cuisine. The restaurant serves a range of regional specialties, including the Frankfurter Würstchen and Handkäse mit Musik. Visitors can also sample the restaurant's signature apple wine, served in traditional blue and white pottery pitchers. Prices are reasonable, with main dishes starting at around €10. Suggested items from the menu include the Apfelwein Wagnerplatte, a platter of regional specialties, and the Rindswurst mit Sauerkraut, a hearty sausage dish. Website: https://www.apfelwein-wagner.com/

2. Kleinmarkthalle Café

Located inside the bustling Kleinmarkthalle food market, this café is a great place to stop for a quick bite while exploring the market's offerings. The café serves a range of sandwiches, salads, and pastries, made with fresh and locally sourced ingredients. Prices are reasonable, with sandwiches starting at around €5. Suggested items from the menu include the Hausgemachte Frikadelle sandwich, made with a traditional German meatball, and the Obstsalat, a fresh fruit salad. Website: https://www.kleinmarkthalle-cafe.de/

3. Seven Swans

This upscale restaurant in Frankfurt's trendy Bahnhofsviertel neighborhood offers a modern take on traditional German cuisine. The restaurant's menu features a range of innovative and creative dishes, made with local and seasonal ingredients. Prices are on the higher side, with main dishes starting at around €25. Suggested items from the menu include the Hausgemachte Wurst, a house-made sausage dish, and the Geschmortes Rind, a slow-cooked beef dish. Website: https://sevenswans.de/

4. Atschel

This rustic and cozy restaurant in the Sachsenhausen neighborhood is a great place to experience traditional Frankfurt cuisine. The restaurant serves a range of hearty dishes, including the famous Rippchen mit Kraut, a dish of cured pork ribs and sauerkraut. Prices are reasonable, with main dishes starting at around €15. Suggested items from the menu include the Apfelwein-Bratwurst, a sausage dish made with apple wine, and the Handkäse mit Musik. Website: https://www.atschel-frankfurt.de/

5. Café Hauptwache

This café, located in the heart of Frankfurt's city center, is a great place to stop for a coffee or light meal while exploring the city. The café serves a range of sandwiches, salads, and pastries, as well as a selection of specialty coffees and teas. Prices are reasonable, with sandwiches starting at around €5. Suggested items from the menu include the Panini with goat cheese and the homemade quiche. Website: https://www.cafe-hauptwache.de/

6. O'Reilly's Irish Pub

This cozy pub in the Altstadt neighborhood is a great place to relax with a pint of beer and some classic pub food. The pub serves a range of Irish and international beers, as well as hearty dishes like fish and chips and shepherd's pie. Prices are reasonable, with main dishes starting at around €10. Suggested items from the menu include the Irish Stew and the classic burger. Website: https://oreillys.com/frankfurt/

7. Vevay

This stylish restaurant in the Westend neighborhood offers a fusion of Swiss and Mediterranean cuisine. The menu features a range of innovative dishes, made with fresh and seasonal ingredients. Prices are on the higher side, with main dishes starting at around €20. Suggested items from the menu include the Zürcher Geschnetzeltes, a traditional Swiss dish of sliced veal in a creamy sauce, and the grilled octopus. Website: https://vevay.de/

8. Café Laumer

This traditional café in the Sachsenhausen neighborhood has been serving coffee and pastries for over 100 years. The café's interior features ornate decor and a cozy atmosphere, making it a great place to relax with a cup of coffee and a sweet treat. Prices are reasonable, with pastries starting at around €2. Suggested items from the menu include the Frankfurter Kranz, a traditional cake made with buttercream and cherries, and the apple strudel. Website: http://www.cafe-laumer.de/

9. Maxie Eisen

This trendy restaurant in the Bahnhofsviertel neighborhood serves up Jewish-American comfort food with a modern twist. The menu features a range of creative dishes, from matzo ball soup to pastrami sandwiches. Prices are on the higher side, with main dishes starting at around €20. Suggested items from the menu include the Reuben sandwich and the beef brisket. Website: https://www.maxieeisen.com/

10. Apfelwein Dax

This traditional apple wine tavern in the Bornheim neighborhood is a great place to sample the local specialty. The tavern serves a range of regional dishes, including the famous Handkäse mit Musik and Rippchen mit Kraut. Prices are reasonable, with main dishes starting at around €10. Suggested items from the menu include the Hausmacher Wurst, a homemade sausage dish, and the Schäufele, a slow-cooked pork shoulder. Website: https://www.apfelwein-dax.de/

Frankfurt's Nightlife

Frankfurt is a city that comes to life after dark, with a lively and diverse nightlife scene that offers something for everyone. From trendy bars and clubs to live music venues and late-night eateries, the city has plenty of options for those looking to enjoy a night out.

One of the most popular neighborhoods for nightlife in Frankfurt is the Sachsenhausen district, which is home to a range of traditional apple wine taverns, or Apfelweinlokale. These cozy and rustic taverns serve up local specialties like Handkäse mit Musik and Rippchen mit Kraut, along with the famous local apple wine, known as Apfelwein. Some of the most popular Apfelwein taverns include Dauth-Schneider, Lorsbacher Thal, and Apfelwein Wagner.

For those looking for a more upscale nightlife experience, the Bahnhofsviertel neighborhood is a great place to start. This trendy and cosmopolitan district is home to a range of bars and clubs, offering everything from craft cocktails to live music and DJ sets. Some of the most popular venues include Kinly Bar, The Kinly Rooftop Bar, and O'Reilly's Irish Pub.

If you're in the mood for live music, the Bockenheim and Nordend neighborhoods are great places to explore. These areas are home to a range of venues, from small jazz clubs to larger concert halls, offering everything from local bands to international acts. Some of the most popular venues include Jazzkeller, Batschkapp, and Das Bett.

Finally, for those looking for a late-night bite to eat, the city's many street food markets and eateries are a great option. From the famous Frankfurt Currywurst to Turkish kebabs and Vietnamese pho, there are plenty of options for those looking to satisfy their hunger after a night out on the town.

Overall, Frankfurt's nightlife scene is diverse and vibrant, offering a range of options for those looking to enjoy a night out in the city. Whether you're in the mood for a traditional apple wine tavern, a trendy cocktail bar, or a live music venue, there's something for everyone in this exciting and cosmopolitan city.

V. Shopping in Frankfurt

Frankfurt is a great destination for shoppers, offering a range of options from high-end boutiques to trendy vintage shops and local markets. The city's shopping scene is diverse and vibrant, reflecting its position as a cultural and economic hub of the region.

From the city's modern shopping malls to its charming pedestrian streets, there is something for everyone in Frankfurt's shopping districts. Visitors can explore the city's many luxury brands, from international names like Louis Vuitton and Gucci to local designers and up-and-coming labels. For those looking for more affordable options, the city's many second-hand shops and flea markets offer a range of unique and one-of-a-kind finds.

In addition to its fashion offerings, Frankfurt is also home to a range of specialty shops and markets, offering everything from gourmet food and wine to handmade crafts and artisanal products. Visitors can explore the city's many street markets and food halls, sampling local specialties like cured meats and cheeses, fresh produce, and traditional baked goods.

Overall, Frankfurt's shopping scene is a reflection of the city's cosmopolitan and diverse character, offering a range of options for those looking to explore its cultural and commercial offerings. Whether you're looking for high-end fashion or unique local finds, there is something for everyone in this vibrant and exciting city.

Zeil Shopping District

Zeil is one of the most popular shopping districts in Frankfurt, known for its wide range of fashion and specialty stores. The pedestrian street stretches for over a kilometer, offering a mix of international brands and local shops.

For high-end shopping, visitors can explore the street's luxury brands, including Louis Vuitton, Gucci, and Prada, as well as German designers like Escada and Hugo Boss. There are also a range of mid-priced and affordable stores, including H&M, Zara, and Primark, as well as sports and outdoor brands like Adidas and The North Face.

In addition to its fashion offerings, Zeil is also home to a range of specialty shops and markets. Visitors can explore the Zeilgalerie, a modern shopping mall with a range of restaurants, cafes, and stores selling everything from electronics to jewelry. The street is also home to the weekly Zeilmarkt, a popular flea market offering a range of vintage and second-hand finds.

For those looking for a break from shopping, there are plenty of options for food and drink along Zeil. Visitors can explore the street's many cafes, bars, and restaurants, offering everything from traditional German cuisine to international flavors and trendy cocktails.

Overall, Zeil is a great destination for shoppers looking to explore Frankfurt's fashion and retail offerings. With a mix of luxury and affordable brands, specialty stores, and local markets, there is something for everyone in this bustling and exciting shopping district.

MyZeil Shopping Center

MyZeil is a modern shopping center located in the heart of Frankfurt's Zeil shopping district. The center features a unique and striking design, with a glass facade and a spiraling atrium that provides plenty of natural light and an airy atmosphere.

The center is home to over 100 stores, offering a mix of international brands and local shops. Visitors can explore the center's fashion offerings, which include luxury brands like Tommy

Hilfiger and Calvin Klein, as well as popular retailers like H&M and Zara. There are also a range of specialty stores, selling everything from electronics and beauty products to books and toys.

In addition to its retail offerings, MyZeil is also home to a range of dining options. The center features a food court with a range of international cuisines, including Asian, Italian, and Mexican. There are also a number of cafes and restaurants throughout the center, offering everything from coffee and pastries to full meals.

One of the highlights of MyZeil is its rooftop terrace, offering panoramic views of the city skyline. Visitors can enjoy a drink or a snack while taking in the views, or relax in one of the center's comfortable seating areas.

Overall, MyZeil is a great destination for shoppers looking for a modern and stylish shopping experience. With a range of stores and dining options, as well as its unique design and rooftop terrace, the center is a must-visit for anyone exploring Frankfurt's shopping district.

Berger Street Shopping

Berger Street is a popular shopping destination in Frankfurt's trendy Bornheim neighborhood. The street features a mix of independent boutiques and specialty stores, offering a range of unique and one-of-a-kind finds.

One of the highlights of shopping on Berger Street is its focus on sustainability and ethical fashion. Many of the boutiques feature local designers and brands that use sustainable materials and production methods, offering a range of eco-friendly and socially responsible options. Visitors can explore stores like Goldmarie, offering sustainable and organic clothing, and Lanius, a local brand that focuses on fair trade and sustainable fashion.

In addition to its fashion offerings, Berger Street is also home to a range of specialty stores and markets. Visitors can explore the weekly Bornheim Markt, a popular farmer's market offering fresh produce, baked goods, and artisanal products. The street is also home to a range of specialty stores, including bookstores, toy shops, and home decor stores.

For those looking for a break from shopping, Berger Street is also home to a range of cafes and restaurants. Visitors can enjoy a coffee or a snack at one of the street's many cafes, or enjoy a meal at one of its trendy restaurants, like Apfelwein Klein or Pizzeria Montana.

Overall, Berger Street is a great destination for shoppers looking to explore Frankfurt's independent and sustainable fashion offerings. With a mix of boutique stores and specialty markets, as well as a range of dining options, the street is a must-visit for anyone looking to experience the city's unique and creative character.

Traditional Markets and Souvenirs

Traditional Markets and Souvenirs:

Frankfurt is known for its traditional markets, offering a range of local specialties and unique souvenirs. Visitors can explore the city's many markets, from the weekly farmer's markets to the seasonal Christmas markets, to find a range of unique and one-of-a-kind finds.

One of the most popular markets in Frankfurt is the weekly Saturday market at Konstablerwache. The market offers a range of fresh produce, flowers, and artisanal products, as well as street food stalls selling everything from bratwurst to crepes. Visitors can also explore the nearby Zeil market, offering a range of handmade crafts and souvenirs.

For those looking for a taste of local specialties, the Kleinmarkthalle is a must-visit. This indoor market offers a range of regional products, including cured meats, cheeses, and baked goods. Visitors can sample local specialties like Handkäse mit Musik, a traditional cheese dish, and Grüne Soße, a local herb sauce.

Frankfurt is also known for its Christmas markets, which take place throughout the city during the holiday season. These markets offer a range of festive decorations, handmade crafts, and local food and drink specialties. The most famous of these markets is the Frankfurt Christmas Market, which takes place in the city's historic Römerberg square.

In addition to its traditional markets, Frankfurt also offers a range of souvenir shops and stores. Visitors can explore stores like Kaufhaus Hessen, offering a range of local products and souvenirs, or the Frankfurt Airport Shop, offering a range of duty-free products and gifts.

Overall, Frankfurt's traditional markets and souvenir shops offer a range of unique and one-of-a-kind finds, reflecting the city's rich cultural and culinary heritage. Whether you're looking for fresh produce, handmade crafts, or local specialties, there's something for everyone in this vibrant and exciting city.

VI. Day Trips from Frankfurt
Heidelberg

Located just an hour south of Frankfurt, Heidelberg is a charming and historic town that makes for a great day trip from the city. The town is known for its picturesque old town, romantic castle, and scenic views of the Neckar River.

One of the highlights of Heidelberg is its historic Old Town, or Altstadt, which features a range of well-preserved Baroque and Gothic buildings. Visitors can explore the town's many narrow streets and squares, stopping to admire historic landmarks like the Heiliggeistkirche, a beautiful church dating back to the 14th century.

Another must-visit attraction in Heidelberg is the town's castle, or Schloss Heidelberg. The castle dates back to the 13th century and features a mix of Gothic and Renaissance architecture. Visitors can explore the castle's many courtyards, towers, and gardens, as well as enjoy panoramic views of the town and surrounding countryside.

For those looking for a break from sightseeing, Heidelberg is also home to a range of cafes, restaurants, and wine bars. Visitors can enjoy a cup of coffee or a glass of local wine while taking in the town's charming atmosphere.

In addition to its cultural offerings, Heidelberg is also a great destination for outdoor enthusiasts. The town is located along the Neckar River, offering plenty of opportunities for hiking, biking, and boating. Visitors can explore the town's many parks and gardens, including the famous Philosophenweg, a scenic hillside path offering panoramic views of the town and river.

Overall, Heidelberg is a great destination for a day trip from Frankfurt, offering a mix of history, culture, and outdoor activities. With its charming old town, romantic castle, and scenic views, the town is a must-visit for anyone exploring the region.

Rhine Valley

The Rhine Valley is a scenic and historic region located just south of Frankfurt. The valley is known for its picturesque towns, medieval castles, and scenic river views, making it a popular destination for day trips from the city.

Here is a suggested daily plan for a day trip to the Rhine Valley:

Morning: Start your day by taking a train or car to the town of Rüdesheim am Rhein, located about an hour west of Frankfurt. Rüdesheim is a charming town known for its historic old town and scenic vineyards. Take a stroll through the town's narrow streets and squares, stopping to admire landmarks like the St. Jakobus Church and the medieval Brömserburg Castle.

Midday: After exploring Rüdesheim, take a scenic boat tour along the Rhine River to the town of Bacharach. The boat tour offers stunning views of the valley's vineyards and castles, as well as a chance to relax and enjoy the scenery. Once you arrive in Bacharach, take a stroll through the town's historic old town, which features well-preserved half-timbered houses and a range of cafes and restaurants.

Afternoon: After lunch in Bacharach, take a short train or car ride to the town of St. Goar, located on the opposite side of the river. St. Goar is known for its stunning medieval castle, Burg Rheinfels, which offers panoramic views of the river and surrounding countryside. Visitors can explore the castle's many rooms and towers, as well as enjoy a drink or snack at the castle's cafe.

Evening: After exploring St. Goar, take a train or car back to Frankfurt, stopping at the town of Bingen am Rhein on the way. Bingen is known for its historic bridge, the Bingen Rhine Bridge, which offers stunning views of the river and valley. Visitors can also explore the town's many parks and gardens, including the famous Rupertsberg Monastery Gardens.

Overall, a day trip to the Rhine Valley offers a mix of history, culture, and scenic views, making it a must-visit destination for anyone exploring the region. With its charming towns, medieval castles, and scenic river views, the valley is a perfect escape from the hustle and bustle of Frankfurt.

The Taunus Mountains

The Taunus Mountains are a scenic and natural region located just north of Frankfurt. The mountains are known for their stunning forests, rolling hills, and quaint towns, making them a popular destination for day trips from the city.

Here is a suggested daily plan for a day trip to the Taunus Mountains:

Morning: Start your day by taking a train or car to the town of Kronberg im Taunus, located about half an hour north of Frankfurt. Kronberg is a charming town known for its well-preserved medieval castle, Schloss Kronberg, which dates back to the 14th century. Take a stroll through the town's historic old town, stopping to admire landmarks like the St. Johanniskirche and the Kronberg Castle Gardens.

Midday: After exploring Kronberg, take a short drive or hike to the nearby town of Königstein im Taunus. Königstein is known for its scenic views of the Taunus Mountains and its historic old town, which features well-preserved half-timbered houses and a range of cafes and restaurants. Visitors can also explore the town's famous castle, the Königstein Fortress, which dates back to the 12th century.

Afternoon: After lunch in Königstein, take a scenic drive or hike through the Taunus Mountains, stopping at one of the many parks and forests along the way. One popular destination is the Opel-Zoo, located in the town of Kronberg, which offers a range of exotic animals and interactive exhibits. Another option is the Taunus Wunderland amusement park, which offers a range of rides and attractions for families and kids.

Evening: After exploring the Taunus Mountains, take a train or car back to Frankfurt, stopping at the town of Bad Homburg on the way. Bad Homburg is known for its historic thermal baths, offering a range of spa treatments and relaxation options. Visitors can also explore the town's many parks and gardens, including the famous Kurpark, which features a range of sculptures and fountains.

Overall, a day trip to the Taunus Mountains offers a mix of nature, culture, and relaxation, making it a must-visit destination for anyone exploring the region. With its charming towns, scenic views, and natural beauty, the mountains are a perfect escape from the city.

Würzburg

Würzburg is a charming and historic town located about two hours east of Frankfurt. The town is known for its well-preserved Baroque architecture, rich cultural heritage, and scenic views of the Main River, making it a popular destination for day trips from the city.

Here is a suggested daily plan for a day trip to Würzburg:

Morning: Start your day by taking a train or car to the town of Würzburg, located on the banks of the Main River. Würzburg is known for its historic old town, which features a range of well-preserved Baroque and Gothic buildings. Take a stroll through the town's many narrow streets and squares, stopping to admire landmarks like the Würzburg Residence, a beautiful palace dating back to the 18th century.

Midday: After exploring Würzburg, take a short walk or drive to the nearby Marienberg Fortress, located on a hill overlooking the town. The fortress dates back to the 13th century and offers stunning views of the Main River and surrounding countryside. Visitors can explore the fortress's many rooms and towers, as well as enjoy a drink or snack at the fortress's cafe.

Afternoon: After lunch at the fortress, take a short train or car ride to the nearby town of Veitshöchheim, located along the Main River. Veitshöchheim is known for its beautiful palace gardens, the Veitshöchheim Palace Gardens, which feature a range of fountains, sculptures, and flower beds. Visitors can explore the gardens on foot or by boat, taking in the scenic views of the river and town.

Evening: After exploring Veitshöchheim, take a train or car back to Würzburg, stopping at the town's many cafes and restaurants along the way. Visitors can enjoy a glass of local wine or beer, as well as sample local specialties like the famous Franconian sausages or the local white wine, Silvaner.

VII. Accommodation in Frankfurt

Frankfurt is a diverse and dynamic city, offering a range of accommodation options for visitors. Whether you're looking for budget-friendly options or luxurious accommodations, there's something for everyone in this vibrant and exciting city.

Best Areas to Stay in Frankfurt:

When it comes to choosing the best area to stay in Frankfurt, there are a few key neighborhoods that stand out. These areas offer a range of accommodation options, as well as easy access to the city's many attractions and cultural offerings.

1. Altstadt (Old Town): The Altstadt is Frankfurt's historic center, offering a range of well-preserved Gothic and Baroque architecture. The area is home to many of the city's cultural landmarks, including the Römerberg, St. Paul's Church, and Frankfurt Cathedral. The Altstadt is also home to a range of hotels and guesthouses, offering a mix of budget-friendly and luxury options.

2. Bahnhofsviertel: Located just south of the city's main train station, the Bahnhofsviertel is a diverse and multicultural neighborhood known for its lively nightlife and trendy restaurants. The area is home to a range of hotels and hostels, offering budget-friendly options for travelers.

3. Sachsenhausen: Located on the south bank of the Main River, Sachsenhausen is a popular neighborhood known for its traditional Apfelwein taverns and lively nightlife. The area is home to a range of hotels and guesthouses, offering a mix of budget-friendly and luxury options.

4. Westend: Located just west of the city center, the Westend is a trendy and upscale neighborhood known for its luxurious homes and high-end boutiques. The area is home to a range of

luxury hotels and apartments, offering a luxurious and sophisticated experience for travelers.

Budget-friendly Accommodation:

Frankfurt offers a range of budget-friendly accommodation options for travelers, including hostels, guesthouses, and budget hotels. These options offer affordable prices and easy access to the city's many attractions and cultural offerings.

1. Five Elements Hostel: Located in the Bahnhofsviertel neighborhood, the Five Elements Hostel offers budget-friendly accommodations for travelers. The hostel features a range of dorms and private rooms, as well as a communal kitchen and lounge area.

2. Meininger Hotel Frankfurt/Main Messe: Located just south of the city center, the Meininger Hotel Frankfurt/Main Messe offers budget-friendly accommodations for travelers. The hotel features a range of private rooms and dorms, as well as a communal kitchen and lounge area.

3. Jugendherberge Frankfurt – Haus der Jugend: Located in the Sachsenhausen neighborhood, the Jugendherberge Frankfurt – Haus der Jugend offers budget-friendly accommodations for travelers. The hostel features a range of dorms and private rooms, as well as a communal kitchen and lounge area.

Luxury Accommodation:

For those looking for a luxurious and sophisticated experience, Frankfurt offers a range of high-end hotels and apartments. These options offer luxurious amenities and easy access to the city's many cultural offerings.

1. Villa Kennedy: Located in the Westend neighborhood, the Villa Kennedy is a luxurious hotel offering a range of high-end

amenities and services. The hotel features a range of rooms and suites, as well as a spa, fitness center, and on-site restaurant.

2. Jumeirah Frankfurt: Located in the city center, the Jumeirah Frankfurt is a luxurious hotel offering a range of high-end amenities and services. The hotel features a range of rooms and suites, as well as a spa, fitness center, and on-site restaurant.

3. The Frankfurt Hotel: Located in the Altstadt neighborhood, The Frankfurt Hotel is a luxurious hotel offering a range of high-end amenities and services. The hotel features a range of rooms and suites, as well as a spa, fitness center, and on-site restaurant. The hotel also features stunning views of the city skyline and easy access to many of Frankfurt's cultural landmarks.

4. Adina Apartment Hotel Frankfurt Neue Oper: Located just west of the city center, the Adina Apartment Hotel Frankfurt Neue Oper offers luxurious apartment-style accommodations for travelers. The hotel features a range of one- and two-bedroom apartments, as well as a fitness center, on-site restaurant, and rooftop terrace.

5. Le Meridien Frankfurt: Located in the city center, Le Meridien Frankfurt is a luxurious hotel offering a range of high-end amenities and services. The hotel features a range of rooms and suites, as well as a spa, fitness center, and on-site restaurant. The hotel also offers stunning views of the city skyline and easy access to many of Frankfurt's cultural landmarks.

VIII. Getting Around Frankfurt

Frankfurt is a well-connected and easily navigable city, offering a range of transportation options for visitors. Whether you prefer public transportation, taxis, or biking, there are plenty of ways to explore the city and its many attractions.

Public Transportation:

Frankfurt's public transportation system is efficient and easy to use, with a range of options including buses, trains, and trams. The city's main transportation hub is the Frankfurt Hauptbahnhof, located in the city center. From here, visitors can take trains and trams to destinations throughout the city and surrounding areas.

The city's public transportation system is operated by RMV, which offers a range of ticket options including single tickets, day passes, and weekly or monthly passes. Tickets can be purchased at ticket machines located at train and tram stations, as well as at many convenience stores and newsstands throughout the city.

Taxis:

Taxis are readily available throughout the city and can be a convenient option for getting around Frankfurt. Taxis in Frankfurt are metered and fares are calculated based on distance traveled and time spent in the taxi. Visitors can hail taxis on the street or call for a pickup using a local taxi app.

Biking in Frankfurt:

Frankfurt is a bike-friendly city, with a range of bike lanes and trails throughout the city and surrounding areas. Biking can be a fun and efficient way to explore the city and its many attractions. Visitors can rent bikes from a range of rental shops throughout the city, as well as from bike sharing programs like Call a Bike and Nextbike.

One popular bike route in Frankfurt is the Main River Greenway, a scenic trail that runs along the Main River and offers stunning views of the city skyline. The trail is well-marked and offers a mix of paved and gravel paths, making it suitable for all skill levels.

Another popular bike route is the Nidda River Trail, a 22-kilometer trail that runs along the Nidda River and offers beautiful views of the surrounding countryside. The trail is well-marked and offers a mix of paved and gravel paths, making it suitable for all skill levels.

Overall, Frankfurt offers a range of transportation options to suit every traveler's needs and preferences. Whether you prefer public transportation, taxis, or biking, there are plenty of ways to explore the city and its many attractions.

IX. Practical Information for Visitors

When traveling to Frankfurt, it's important to be prepared with some practical information to ensure a smooth and enjoyable trip. Here are some key things to keep in mind:

Climate and Weather:

Frankfurt has a temperate climate, with mild summers and cold winters. The best time to visit is from May to September, when the weather is mild and pleasant. During this time, temperatures range from around 15°C to 25°C (59°F to 77°F), with occasional rain showers.

Money and Currency Exchange:

The currency used in Frankfurt is the Euro (€). Visitors can exchange currency at banks and exchange offices located throughout the city, as well as at many hotels and airports. It's important to note that some places, especially smaller shops and restaurants, may only accept cash, so it's a good idea to carry some Euros with you at all times.

Language:

The official language of Frankfurt is German, although many people also speak English. It's always a good idea to learn a few basic German phrases, especially when traveling to more rural areas or smaller towns. Some useful phrases include "Hallo" (hello), "Danke" (thank you), and "Entschuldigung" (excuse me).

Useful Phone Numbers:

In case of an emergency, it's important to know some useful phone numbers to call for help. Here are some important numbers to keep in mind:

- Police: 110
- Fire department: 112

- Ambulance: 112

Other useful phone numbers include:

- Tourist Information: +49 69 2123 8800
- Airport Information: +49 1806 372 4636

Overall, with some basic preparation and knowledge, visitors to Frankfurt can enjoy a smooth and enjoyable trip, taking in all the city has to offer.

3-Day Frankfurt Classics Itinerary:

Day 1

7:00am - Arrival at Frankfurt Airport

Public transportation info:

Frankfurt has a very easy network of trains, buses, subways and railways that will get you anywhere within and outside the city limits. A traveling day-pass will cost 7 Euro and individual rides are quite affordable as well, usually around 2 Euros for a one-way ticket. Except for buses, where you pay directly with the bus driver, you are expected to purchase your ticket ahead a time, most likely at a machine. The system is an honor-system, but you can be stopped and asked to present your ticket at any given time and should be prepared to do so. If not, you'll be fined and that can range anywhere from 50-80 Euros. To get from the airport into the city is very easy and quick, but there are also lots of taxis parked out front and there's no line to get in, as it is the case at some other international airports.

9:00am Arrival at the Hotel

Our recommended hotel is Steigenberger Frankfurter Hof

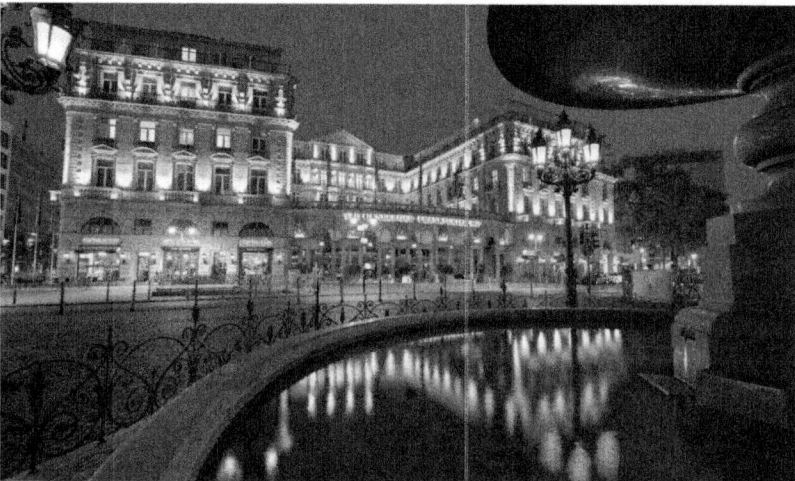

Steigenberger Frankfurter Hof is a luxurious five-star hotel located in the heart of Frankfurt's city center. With its elegant and sophisticated decor, world-class amenities, and prime location, this hotel offers a truly luxurious and memorable stay for visitors to the city.

Pros:

Location: The hotel is located in the heart of Frankfurt's city center, offering easy access to many of the city's top attractions, including the historic old town, the Zeil shopping district, and the Frankfurt Opera House.

Amenities: The hotel offers a range of luxurious amenities, including a spa, fitness center, and rooftop terrace with stunning views of the city skyline.

Dining: The hotel features a range of on-site dining options, including a Michelin-starred restaurant, a bar, and a cafe.

Service: The hotel's staff are known for their exceptional service and attention to detail, ensuring a truly luxurious and comfortable stay for guests.

Cons:

Price: Steigenberger Frankfurter Hof is a luxury hotel and comes with a higher price tag than some other hotels in the city. However, the high-end amenities and exceptional service make it worth the price for those looking for a truly luxurious experience.

Noise: As the hotel is located in the heart of the city, it can be noisy at times, especially during weekends and festivals. However, the hotel offers soundproofed rooms to ensure a comfortable and peaceful stay.

Website: The hotel's website is https://www.steigenberger.com/en/hotels/all-hotels/germany/frankfurt/steigenberger-frankfurter-hof

Address:Steigenberger Frankfurter Hof is located at Am Kaiserplatz, Bethmannstraße 33, 60311 Frankfurt am Main, Germany.

Prices: Room rates at Steigenberger Frankfurter Hof start at around €200 per night for a standard room, with rates for suites and higher-end rooms ranging from €500 to €1,500 per night. Special offers and packages are also available on the hotel's website.

9:30am - Breakfast at Hofgarten Restaurant

You don't have to go far: It's at your hotel! The hotel has multiple, fabulous restaurants and bars inside and since you'll probably be hungry by the time you'll get to check-in, this would be the perfect first stop. The restaurant offers an extensive buffet prepared from the freshest and most popular ingredients.

11:00am - Staedel Museum

The Städel, officially the Städelsches Kunstinstitut und Städtische Galerie, is an art museum in Frankfurt am Main, with one of the most important collections in Germany. This is a lovely museum containing contemporary art, and it's easy to walk through the entire museum within a solid 3 hours. It's definitely worth a trip if you're an art lover and you will surely appreciate its great, impressive collections.

The Städel owns 2,700 paintings (of which 600 are displayed) and a collection of 100,000 drawings and prints as well as 600 sculptures. It has around 4,000 m² of display and a library of 100,000 books and 400 periodicals.

The Städel was honoured as "Museum of the Year 2012" by the German art critics association AICA in 2012. In the same year the museum recorded the highest attendance figures in its history, of 447,395 visitors.

History

The Städel was founded in 1815 by the Frankfurt banker and merchant Johann Friedrich Städel. In 1878, a new building, designed according to the Gründerzeit style, was erected on Schaumainkai street, presently the major museum district. By the start of the 20th century, the gallery was among the most prominent German collections of classic Pan-European art; the other such collections open to the public were the Dresden Gallery, the Alte Pinakothek in Munich, and the Altes Museum in Berlin.

World War II

In 1937, 77 paintings and 700 prints were confiscated from the museum when the National Socialists declared them "degenerate art".

In 1939, the collection was moved out of Frankfurt to protect it from damage in World War II. The collection of the Staedel, officially known as the Städelsches Kunstinstitut und Städtische Galerie of Frankfurt, was removed from the museum to avoid destruction from the Allied bombings, and the collection was stored in the Schloss Rossbach, a castle owned by the Baron Thüngen near Bad Brückenau in Bavaria. There, the museum's paintings and library were discovered by Lt. Thomas Carr Howe, USN, of the American Monuments, Fine Arts and Archives program. Although the Baron von Thüngen and his wife were uncooperative with the Americans, Frau Dr. Holzinger, a licensed physician and the Swiss wife of the Staedel museum director, was present at the site and assisted with the cataloging and the removal of the items to the Munich Central Collecting Point. Lt. Howe said, "The first room to be inspected was a library adjoining the sitting room in which we had been waiting. Here we found a quantity of excellent French Impressionist paintings, all from the permanent collection of the Staedel, and a considerable number of fine Old Master drawings. Most of these were likewise the property of the museum, but a few – I remember one superb Rembrandt sketch – appeared to have come from Switzerland. Those would, of course, have to be looked into later, to determine their exact origin and how they came to be on loan to the museum. But for the moment we were concerned primarily with storage conditions and the problem of security. In another room we found an enormous collection of books, the library of one of the Frankfurt museums. In a third we encountered an array of medieval sculpture – saints all sizes and description, some of carved wood, others of stone, plain or polychromed. These too, were of museum origin. The last storage room was below ground, a vast, cavernous chamber beneath the house. Here was row upon row of pictures, stacked in two tiers down the center of the room and also along two sides. From what we could make of them in the poor light, they were not of high quality. During the summer months they would be alright in the underground room, but we thought the place would be very damp in the winter. Frau Holzinger assured us that this was so and that the pictures should be removed before the bad weather set in."

Renovations

The gallery was substantially damaged by air raids in World War II and it was rebuilt by 1966 following a design by the Frankfurt architect Johannes Krahn. An expansion building for the display of 20th-century work and special exhibits was erected in 1990, designed by the Austrian architect Gustav Peichl. Small structural changes and renovations took place from 1997 to 1999.

The largest extension in the history of the museum intended for the presentation of contemporary art was designed by the Frankfurt architectural firm Schneider+Schumacher and opened in February 2012.

Digital expansion

The Städel is currently significantly enlarging its activities and outreach through a major digital expansion on the occasion of its 200-year anniversary in 2015. Already available to visitors is an exhibition 'digitorial' and free access to WiFi throughout the museum and its grounds. From March the museum will offer to visitors a new Städel app, the possibility of listening to audio guides on their own devices, and a new 'cabinet of digital curiosities'. Several more projects are currently in development including an online exhibition platform; educational computer games for children; online art-history courses and a digital art book.

Collection

The Städel has European paintings from seven centuries, beginning with the early 14th century, moving into Late Gothic, the Renaissance, Baroque, and into the 19th, 20th and 21st centuries. The large collection of prints and drawings is not on permanent display and occupies the first floor of the museum. Works on paper not on display can be viewed by appointment.

The gallery has a conservation department that performs conservation and restoration work on the collection.

Admission: 14 Euros| Hours: 10-21.00. Saturday, Sunday, Tuesday and Wednesday the museum closes at 18.00

Address: Schaumainkai 63 | 60596 Frankfurt, 60596
Frankfurt, Hessen, Germany| Phone Number: +49 69 605098200

Website: www.**staedelmuseum**.de/en

14:00pm - Classico for lunch

Classico is an Italian restaurant located in the heart of Frankfurt's historic old town. With its cozy and inviting atmosphere, high-quality ingredients, and authentic Italian cuisine, this restaurant has become a favorite among locals and visitors alike.

The restaurant's menu features a range of classic Italian dishes, including pasta, pizza, and seafood, as well as a selection of vegetarian and gluten-free options. All dishes are made with high-quality ingredients, many of which are imported directly from Italy, and are prepared fresh to order.

One of the standout dishes at Classico is the pizza, which is made in a traditional wood-fired oven and features a range of delicious toppings, from classic margherita to more creative options like prosciutto and arugula.

The restaurant also offers a range of Italian wines and cocktails to complement the meal, as well as a selection of homemade desserts, including tiramisu and panna cotta.

With its warm and inviting atmosphere, high-quality cuisine, and attentive service, Classico is a must-visit restaurant for anyone looking for a taste of Italy in the heart of Frankfurt.

Website: The restaurant's website is https://www.classico-frankfurt.de/

Address: Classico is located at Liebfrauenberg 39, 60313 Frankfurt am Main, Germany.

Prices: Prices at Classico are reasonable, with pasta dishes starting at around €10 and pizzas starting at around €12. Main courses and seafood dishes range from €15 to €25, and desserts are priced at around €7. The restaurant also offers a lunch menu, as well as special deals on certain days of the week.

15:30pm - Frankfurt Main River Cruise (upstream or downstream)

At 3:30 pm, embark on a scenic Frankfurt Main River Cruise, considered one of the most picturesque ways to see the city from the water. The cruise options include a 50-minute trip upstream or downstream, or a 100-minute journey that covers both directions and all major highlights. Opt for the longer route to make the most of the experience.

Prices for tickets start at $10, and the departure point is at the central "Eiserner Steg" bridge in Frankfurt. Live commentary in German and English is available, providing insightful information about the city's landmarks and history.

The cruise operates from Monday to Saturday, with upstream departures at 12 pm, 2 pm, and 4 pm, and downstream departures at 11 am, 1 pm, 3 pm, and 5 pm. On Sundays and public holidays, the service runs every half-hour between April and October. Upstream departures start at 11:30 am and run until 6 pm, while downstream departures begin at 11 am and continue until 6:30 pm

17:30pm - Walking tour

For this, you don't necessarily need a guide, but the greatest pleasure with this is to explore the riverside on your own and take a stroll along Main River. Frankfurt is quite serene and peaceful in these parts of town and lovely to see towards the end of the day (unless there's a festival going on!).

19:00pm - Drinks at The Parlour

One of the best cocktail lounges in Frankfurt! It's a little pricey, but well worth it and some of the drinks are quite unique. A good spot for a pre-dinner drink, or post-dinner as well, if you choose to come here at a busier, later time. It is a bit awkward for foreigners to get

here specially if the taxi driver does not know the area; make sure you use the building number to find the place as there is no big sign outside

Address: Zwingergasse 6, 60313 Frankfurt, Germany
Phone number: +49 69 90025808| **Hours:** Open from 19.00 to 3.00 in the morning (closed on Sundays)

20:30pm - Dinner at Zenzakan

Zenzakan is a unique restaurant located in the heart of Frankfurt's financial district. With its sophisticated decor, modern fusion cuisine, and inventive cocktails, this restaurant offers a one-of-a-kind dining experience.

The restaurant's menu features a range of dishes that blend Asian and European flavors, using high-quality ingredients and creative presentation to create dishes that are both visually stunning and delicious. Popular menu items include the sushi rolls, crispy duck, and wagyu beef.

In addition to its food, Zenzakan is known for its inventive cocktails, which blend traditional Asian ingredients with modern mixology techniques. The bar also offers an extensive wine and sake list, as well as a range of beer and spirits.

The restaurant's decor is sleek and modern, with a blend of Asian and European influences. The space features an open kitchen, a bar area, and a main dining room with plenty of seating options.

The restaurant's website is
https://www.zenzakan.de/en/home-en/

Address:Zenzakan is located at Taunusanlage 15, 60325 Frankfurt am Main, Germany.

Prices: Prices at Zenzakan are in the higher range, with starters priced at around €15 and main courses ranging from €20 to €50. Cocktails and other drinks start at around €12. The restaurant also offers a range of tasting menus and special offers, as well as private dining options.

1st Day Map

Below you can find the map with all the places for your first day in Frankfurt. To get this map online, you can click here. This link will open the map for you in Google maps, so that you can easily navigate around in the city.

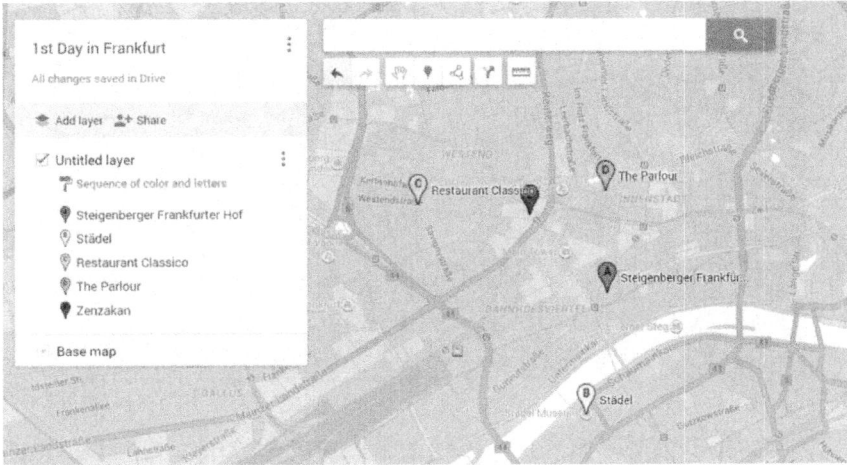

Day 2

9:30am – Breakfast at Zeil Street (MyZeil)

The "Zeil" is the main shopping area in Frankfurt. On the way from your hotel to this destination, you will encounter countless breakfast places, as well as in any of the side streets, where you'll often find a hidden gem. Afterwards, all the shops will be open, so feel free to do some shopping and looking-around.

A little side note: A typical German breakfast consists of some type of bread (usually rolls or crusty bread), with cheese, cold cuts and marmalade.

12:00am - Roemer/Roemerplatz

Located in a famous, historical town square in Frankfurt, in walking distance from the shopping street, this important landmark shows you true and typical German architecture. This town square is also where the annual Christmas market takes place and is the center of many festivals and celebrations throughout the year. There are several souvenir shops, if you're looking for presents for loved ones back home, and some very yummy ice cream parlors, worth trying out.

Address: Römerberg 27, 60311 Frankfurt am Main, Germany| tel: +49 69 21201

13:00pm - Weinstube im Roemer
At 1:00 pm, head to Weinstube im Roemer for an introduction to traditional German hospitality and cuisine. The restaurant offers generous portions at moderate prices, making it an excellent choice for visitors to the old part of town.

The menu features classic German dishes, including sausages, schnitzel, and sauerkraut, as well as a range of local wines and beers. The restaurant's cozy interior and friendly staff make for a welcoming atmosphere, perfect for a relaxed lunch or dinner.

Weinstube im Roemer is located in Frankfurt-Altstadt at Römerberg 19, Frankfurt, Hessen, Germany, and can be reached at 069-

291331. The restaurant's opening hours are Sunday from 11:30 am to 11:00 pm, Tuesday to Friday from 4:00 pm to 11:00 pm, and Saturday from 11:30 am to 11:00 pm.

14:30pm - Palmengarten

At 2:30 pm, head to the serene and beautiful Palmengarten, one of the largest botanical gardens in Germany. With its diverse collection of plants from all over the world, the garden offers a peaceful and educational experience for visitors of all ages.

Plan to spend about 1-2 hours exploring the various themed gardens, including a rose garden, a Mediterranean garden, and a tropical rainforest greenhouse. There are also several ponds and fountains throughout the garden, providing a tranquil setting to relax and enjoy nature.

The Palmengarten is located at Siesmayerstr. 61, 60323 Frankfurt, Hessen, Germany, and can be reached at 069 2123 3939. Admission prices are 7 Euros for adults and 2 Euros for children up to 13 years old. The garden is open from 9:00 am to 6:00 pm.

16:30pm - Chinese Garden

A trip to China without getting on a plane! It's a very pretty, but also small garden and you can easily walk it all through within an hour. It contains a little waterfall, which is quite lovely.

Address: Friedberger Tor | Chinesischer Garten, 60311Frankfurt, Hessen, Germany

Opening hours: Weekdays it opens at 7 through nightfall; Weekends it opens at 10, also through nightfall.

18:00pm - Dinner at Restaurant Francais

At 6:00 pm, treat yourself to an unforgettable culinary experience with dinner at Restaurant Francais, located within the luxurious Steigenberger Frankfurter Hof hotel. This award-winning restaurant is renowned for its French cuisine, earning critical acclaim and a loyal following of foodies.

Indulge in the finest French cuisine, with a menu that features a range of classic and modern dishes, crafted with the highest-quality ingredients and presented with artistry. The restaurant's elegant decor and impeccable service create a sophisticated and memorable atmosphere for a special occasion or romantic dinner.

As one of the most sought-after dining destinations in Frankfurt, reservations are highly recommended. Whether you are a gourmet food lover or simply looking for an exceptional dining experience, Restaurant Francais is sure to exceed your expectations.

Restaurant Francais is open from Tuesday to Friday for lunch from 12:00 pm to 1:45 pm and for dinner from Tuesday to Saturday from 6:30 pm to 9:30 pm.

If you're a guest at the Steigenberger Frankfurter Hof hotel, this restaurant is a must-visit. But even if you're staying elsewhere, it's worth making the trip to experience one of the best French restaurants in Frankfurt.

20:00pm - Alte Oper

At 8:00 pm, immerse yourself in the world of art and culture with a visit to Alte Oper. This magnificent concert hall, located in the heart of Frankfurt, is a cultural hub that hosts a wide range of performances, including classical music, opera, ballet, and theater.

Check the schedule beforehand to see what performances are on offer. Most shows start at 8:00 pm, and the program changes regularly, offering something for every taste. Attending a performance at the Alte Oper is truly a unique experience, and a must-do activity for art and music enthusiasts.

The concert hall is located at Opernplatz 1, 60313 Frankfurt am Main, Germany, and can be reached at +49 69 13400. Ticket prices vary depending on the performance, but they are generally very affordable. Discounts are available for students, Frankfurt Pass-holders, the unemployed, and other categories. It's recommended to book tickets in advance, as performances often sell out quickly.

The Alte Oper is not only a place for performances, but also offers guided tours of the building. You can explore the various halls and spaces, learn about the history of the building, and see behind the scenes of the performances.

Before or after the show, you can also enjoy a drink or a meal at one of the on-site restaurants or bars, which offer a range of cuisines and atmospheres to suit every taste.

In summary, Alte Oper is a must-visit destination for anyone interested in culture and the arts. With its impressive architecture, diverse programming, and affordable prices, it's a great way to experience the best of Frankfurt's cultural scene.

2nd Day Map

Welcome to the second day of your Frankfurt adventure! Today's itinerary will take you to some of the city's most iconic landmarks and hidden gems, giving you a deeper understanding of Frankfurt's rich culture, history, and cuisine.

To help you navigate your way through the city, we've created a customized Google map with all the spots on today's itinerary marked out for you. You can access the map on your phone or device, and use it to guide you from one location to the next.

Whether you're a first-time visitor or a seasoned traveler, we're confident that today's itinerary will provide you with an unforgettable Frankfurt experience. So grab your comfortable shoes, your sense of adventure, and let's get started!

Click Here to get this map online.

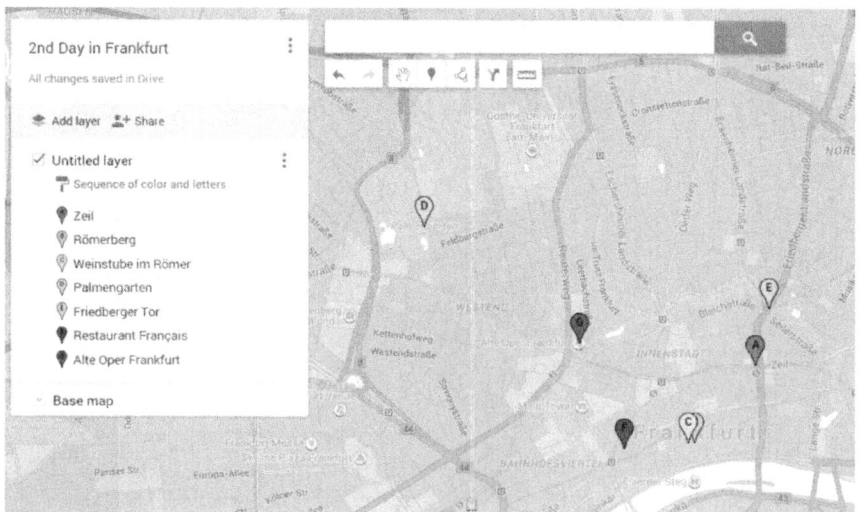

Day 3

9:00am - Café Karin for breakfast

At 9:00 am, start your day off right with a delicious breakfast at Café Karin. This cozy and welcoming breakfast spot offers a range of tasty options at very reasonable prices.

Whether you prefer a classic American breakfast or a traditional English breakfast, Café Karin has something for everyone. The menu includes a variety of freshly made pastries, bread, eggs, and other breakfast favorites, as well as coffee and tea to kickstart your day.

The friendly and courteous service at Café Karin will make you feel right at home, and the cozy atmosphere is the perfect setting for a relaxed and enjoyable breakfast experience.

Café Karin is located at Großer Hirschgraben 28, 60311 Frankfurt, Germany, and can be reached at +49 69 295217. It's recommended to arrive early, as the café can get busy during peak breakfast hours.

Start your day off on the right foot with a tasty breakfast at Café Karin, and get ready for another exciting day exploring the sights and sounds of Frankfurt.

10:00am - Frankfurt Zoo

At 10:00 am, head to the Frankfurt Zoo, one of the oldest zoos in Germany, established in 1858. The zoo is home to a diverse range of fauna, including exotic animals from around the world.

Plan to spend at least 2-3 hours exploring the zoo, which is spread across 11 hectares of land. Be sure to check the feeding schedule for the animals, as it's a fascinating experience to watch them enjoy their meals.

The Frankfurt Zoo is located at Bernhard-Grzimek-Allee 1, 60316 Frankfurt, Hessen, Germany, and can be reached at +69 21233735. It's open from 9:00 am to 5:00 pm, and admission prices are 10 Euros per adult and 5 Euros for a child under the age of 18. Family day passes are available for 25 Euros (2 adults and up to 4 children), and several other discounts are offered for eligible visitors.

In addition to observing the animals, the Frankfurt Zoo offers a range of other experiences, including a children's zoo, a petting zoo, and various playgrounds. There are also several restaurants and cafes on site, offering a range of refreshments and meals.

Before you go, it's recommended to check the zoo's website for any special events or exhibitions that may be taking place during your visit. With so much to see and do, the Frankfurt Zoo is a must-visit destination for families, animal lovers, and anyone looking for a fun and educational experience in Frankfurt.

13:00pm - Ristorante Leon D'Oro for lunch

At 1:00 pm, take a break from your busy day and treat yourself to a delicious lunch at Ristorante Leon D'Oro. This Italian restaurant is located within walking distance of the Frankfurt Zoo, making it a convenient spot to refuel after a morning of exploring.

Ristorante Leon D'Oro is known for its authentic, mouth-watering Italian cuisine and traditional ambiance. The menu includes a range of classic pasta dishes, pizzas, and other Italian favorites, all made with fresh ingredients and cooked to perfection.

The restaurant's warm and welcoming atmosphere provides the perfect setting for a leisurely lunch break. Whether you're dining alone, with friends, or with family, you're sure to enjoy the delicious food and friendly service at Ristorante Leon D'Oro.

The restaurant is located at Waldschmidtstrasse 30, at the corner of Wittelsbacherallee, and can be reached at +069439769. It's open daily from 12:00 pm to 11:30 pm, so you can stop by for lunch or dinner at your convenience.

After a satisfying lunch, you'll be ready to continue your exploration of Frankfurt's many attractions.

14:30pm - German Film Museum

At 2:30 pm, head to the German Film Museum for a fascinating glimpse into the world of filmmaking. This museum is a must-visit destination for film enthusiasts, and offers a range of interactive exhibits that allow you to learn about the history of cinema and the process of making movies.

Plan to spend 1-2 hours exploring the museum, which features a range of displays and exhibits showcasing classic films, movie props, and filmmaking equipment. You'll have the opportunity to interact with film-making tools and even create your own short movie in the museum's interactive studio.

The German Film Museum is located at Schaumainkai 41, 60596 Frankfurt, Hessen, Germany, and can be reached at +49 69 96 12 20 0 or +069 234353. It's open daily from 10:00 am to 6:00 pm, and on Wednesdays, it stays open until 8:00 pm.

Admission prices vary depending on the exhibits you want to see, with the highest entrance fee being 6 Euros. However, discounts apply, and children under 6 get in for free.

Whether you're a fan of classic cinema or interested in the process of making movies, the German Film Museum offers a unique and informative experience that you won't want to miss.

16:00pm - Cathedral of St. Bartholomew

This is a significant, historic church with amazing interior. There's no entrance fee and recommend time is 1-2 hours. It used to serve for the coronation of Holy Roman emperors. The viewing platform on top of the tower is pretty nice and worth the sight, if you are physically in good condition and able to walk up the stairs.

18:00pm - Kabuki for dinner

At 6:00 pm, head to Kabuki, one of the best Japanese restaurants in Frankfurt, located conveniently within walking distance of the English Theatre. With its generous portions and exquisite flavors, this restaurant is a must-visit destination for anyone looking for a memorable dining experience.

The menu at Kabuki features a range of classic Japanese dishes, including sushi, sashimi, and tempura, as well as a variety of grilled meats and seafood. The restaurant also offers a range of vegetarian and gluten-free options, making it a great choice for diners with dietary restrictions.

Kabuki is located at Kaiserstrasse 42, 60329 Frankfurt, Hesse, Germany, and is easily accessible via public transportation or on foot. The restaurant is open for dinner every day, and reservations are highly recommended to ensure you get a table.

Whether you're looking for a romantic dinner for two or a fun night out with friends, Kabuki is sure to impress with its exceptional food and cozy atmosphere. After dinner, why not catch a show at the nearby English Theatre for a perfect end to your evening in Frankfurt?

20:00pm - English Theatre

At 8:00 pm, head to the English Theatre in Frankfurt for an unforgettable evening of entertainment. Check the calendar for upcoming performances and book your tickets in advance to ensure you get a seat for one of their fantastic shows.

The prices are modest, and the shows are always top-notch, featuring talented actors and impressive productions.

The theatre itself is located at Gallusanlage 7, 60329 Frankfurt, Hessen, Germany, and features comfortable seating and a cozy bar where you can relax before the show begins.

Whether you're a theater buff or just looking for a fun night out, the English Theatre offers an exciting and memorable experience that's not to be missed. So don't hesitate to check their schedule and book your tickets today!

Frankfurt's Cultural Treasures Itinerary: Museums, Galleries, and Theatres

Day 1:

9:00 AM - Breakfast at Cafe Hauptwache Start your day with a delicious breakfast at the historic Café Hauptwache, located in the heart of Frankfurt. Enjoy a variety of traditional German pastries and a steaming cup of coffee in this iconic 18th-century building. Address: An der Hauptwache 15, 60313 Frankfurt am Main Website: http://www.cafehauptwache.de/ Price Range: €5-€15

10:00 AM - Städel Museum Take a leisurely 15-minute walk or hop on the U-Bahn (U1, U2, U3, U8) to Schweizer Platz, and then it's just a short walk to the Städel Museum. This prestigious art museum houses a vast collection of European masterpieces from the 14th century to the present day, including works by Rembrandt, Vermeer, and Botticelli. Address: Schaumainkai 63, 60596 Frankfurt am Main Website: https://www.staedelmuseum.de/ Admission: €14 for adults, €10 for students, free for children under 12 Tip: Purchase tickets online in advance to avoid lines.

12:30 PM - Lunch at Holbein's Café-Restaurant Located within the Städel Museum, Holbein's Café-Restaurant offers a selection of delicious meals, from light bites to hearty German dishes. Enjoy your lunch overlooking the museum's beautiful garden. Website: https://www.holbeins.de/ Price Range: €10-€25

2:00 PM - Museum Angewandte Kunst (Museum of Applied Arts) A short 10-minute walk will bring you to the Museum Angewandte

Kunst, a contemporary space dedicated to showcasing design, fashion, and applied arts from various time periods and cultures. Explore thought-provoking exhibitions and installations that challenge the boundaries of art and design. Address: Schaumainkai 17, 60594 Frankfurt am Main Website: https://www.museumangewandtekunst.de/ Admission: €12 for adults, €6 for students, free for children under 12

4:00 PM - Museum für Moderne Kunst (Museum of Modern Art) Head to the Museum für Moderne Kunst by taking the tram (line 15 or 16) to Dom/Römer station. This striking triangular building, often referred to as the "slice of cake," houses an impressive collection of modern and contemporary art from the 1960s to the present day, featuring works by renowned artists such as Andy Warhol, Roy Lichtenstein, and Gerhard Richter. Address: Domstraße 10, 60311 Frankfurt am Main Website: https://www.mmk.art/en/ Admission: €12 for adults, €6 for students, free for children under 12

6:00 PM - Dinner at Zum Gemalten Haus Take the U-Bahn (U4) to Schäfflestraße, and then it's just a short walk to Zum Gemalten Haus. Located in the heart of the historic Sachsenhausen district, this traditional Apfelwein tavern is the perfect place to experience authentic Frankfurt cuisine. Try local dishes such as Grüne Soße (green sauce) and Frankfurter Schnitzel, and don't miss the famous Apfelwein (apple wine). Address: Schweizer Str. 67, 60594 Frankfurt am

Main Website: http://www.zumgemaltenhaus.de

Price Range: €15-€30

8:00 PM - Alte Oper (Old Opera House) Head back to the city center by taking the U-Bahn (U1, U2, U3, U8) to Willy-Brandt-Platz. A short walk away is the Alte Oper, Frankfurt's beautifully restored 19th-century opera house. Check the schedule and book tickets in advance to enjoy a world-class performance of opera, ballet, or classical music. Address: Opernplatz 1, 60313 Frankfurt am Main

Website: https://www.alteoper.de/en/ Admission: Prices vary depending on the performance, from €25 to over €100 Tip: Dress code for performances is typically semi-formal to formal.

Day 2:

9:00 AM - Breakfast at Cafe Karin Begin your second day in Frankfurt with breakfast at the cozy Café Karin, known for its excellent coffee and homemade cakes. Savor a traditional German breakfast or indulge in one of their delicious omelettes. Address: Großer Hirschgraben 28, 60311 Frankfurt am Main Website: http://www.cafekarin.de/ Price Range: €5-€15

10:00 AM - Schirn Kunsthalle Frankfurt Just a 5-minute walk from Café Karin, the Schirn Kunsthalle Frankfurt is one of Germany's leading contemporary art institutions. Explore thought-provoking exhibitions by both established and emerging artists from around the world. Address: Römerberg, 60311 Frankfurt am Main Website: https://www.schirn.de/en/ Admission: €12 for adults, €8 for students, free for children under 12

12:00 PM - Lunch at Klosterhof Located a short walk from the Schirn Kunsthalle, Klosterhof is a charming restaurant offering a mix of traditional German and international cuisine. Enjoy your lunch in their beautiful courtyard garden or cozy indoor seating area. Address: Brückenstraße 10, 60594 Frankfurt am Main Website: https://www.klosterhof-frankfurt.de/ Price Range: €10-€25

2:00 PM - German Film Museum (Deutsches Filmmuseum) After lunch, take the tram (line 14 or 18) to the Deutsches Filmmuseum, a museum dedicated to the art and history of film. Explore engaging exhibitions that showcase the evolution of the film industry, from its earliest beginnings to modern digital technology. Address: Schaumainkai 41, 60596 Frankfurt am Main Website: https://www.deutsches-filminstitut.de/en/filmmuseum/ Admission: €6 for adults, €4 for students, free for children under 12

4:00 PM - English Theatre Frankfurt Take the U-Bahn (U4) to Willy-Brandt-Platz and walk for 10 minutes to the English Theatre Frankfurt, the largest English-speaking theater in continental Europe. Enjoy a matinee performance of a play or musical, performed by talented actors from all over the world. Address: Gallusanlage 7, 60329 Frankfurt am Main Website: https://www.english-theatre.de/ Admission: Prices vary depending on the performance, from €25 to over €60 Tip: Book tickets in advance, as popular shows can sell out quickly.

6:30 PM - Dinner at Apfelwein Wagner Located in the Sachsenhausen district, Apfelwein Wagner is another traditional tavern where you can enjoy authentic Frankfurt cuisine and the famous apple wine. Try their Handkäs mit Musik (cheese marinated in vinegar and onions) or Rippchen mit Kraut (pork ribs with sauerkraut) for a true taste of Frankfurt. Address: Schweizer Str. 71, 60594 Frankfurt am Main Website: https://www.apfelwein-wagner.com/ Price Range: €15-€30

8:30 PM - Frankfurt LAB End your cultural journey in Frankfurt at the Frankfurt LAB, a unique performance and exhibition space dedicated to contemporary performing arts, including dance, theater, and experimental music. Check their schedule for cutting-edge performances that will leave you inspired. Address: Schmidtstraße 12, 60326 Frankfurt am Main Website: https://www.frankfurt-lab.org/en/ Admission: Prices vary depending on the performance, from €15 to over €50 Tip: Some performances may have limited seating or require reservations, so check the website in advance.

Throughout this two-day itinerary, you'll explore the rich cultural treasures of Frankfurt, including museums, galleries, and theaters. The city's excellent public transportation system, consisting of U-Bahn, S-Bahn, trams, and buses, will make it easy for you to navigate from one destination to the next. Remember to validate your ticket before boarding to avoid fines.

Enjoy your journey through Frankfurt's Cultural Treasures and immerse yourself in the vibrant arts scene this dynamic city has to offer!

Historic Frankfurt Itinerary: Walking Tour Through Time

Day 1:

9:00 AM - Breakfast at Café Laumer Start your day with a delicious breakfast at Café Laumer, a traditional German café known for its exquisite pastries, bread, and coffee. Indulge in a variety of breakfast options, including classic German fare and international dishes. Address: Bockenheimer Landstraße 67, 60325 Frankfurt am Main Website: https://www.cafe-laumer.de/en/ Price Range: €5-€15

10:00 AM - Palmengarten (Palm Garden) After breakfast, take a leisurely 10-minute walk to the Palmengarten, a beautiful 19th-century botanical garden that showcases a diverse range of plants from around the world. Explore the various greenhouses and themed gardens while soaking in the history and natural beauty of this urban oasis. Address: Siesmayerstraße 61, 60323 Frankfurt am Main Website: https://palmengarten.de/en/ Admission: €7 for adults, €2 for children (ages 6-13)

12:00 PM - Alte Oper (Old Opera House) Head east towards the city center, either on foot (25 minutes) or by taking the U-Bahn (U6 or U7) to Alte Oper station. The Alte Oper, a magnificent 19th-century opera house, was meticulously restored after being heavily damaged during World War II. Marvel at the stunning architecture and learn about the building's rich history. Address: Opernplatz 1, 60313 Frankfurt am Main Website: https://www.alteoper.de/en/

1:00 PM - Lunch at Vini da Sabatini Just a few steps from the Alte Oper, Vini da Sabatini is a charming Italian restaurant offering a delicious selection of pasta, pizza, and other Italian dishes. Enjoy a leisurely lunch on their outdoor terrace or in the cozy interior. Address: Taubenstraße 3, 60313 Frankfurt am Main Website: https://www.vinidasabatini.de/ Price Range: €10-€25

2:00 PM - Eschenheimer Turm (Eschenheim Tower) After lunch, walk for 10 minutes to reach Eschenheimer Turm, a well-preserved medieval tower that once formed part of Frankfurt's city walls. This 15th-century structure is the oldest and tallest of the city's remaining fortifications, offering a fascinating glimpse into Frankfurt's past. Address: Eschenheimer Tor 1, 60318 Frankfurt am Main

3:00 PM - St. Paul's Church (Paulskirche) Head south for about 10 minutes to reach St. Paul's Church, a significant site in German history. This 18th-century church was the meeting place of the Frankfurt Parliament in 1848, Germany's first freely elected legislative body. Explore the church's beautiful interior and learn about its historical significance through informative exhibits. Address: Paulsplatz 11, 60311 Frankfurt am Main

4:00 PM - Römerberg (Roman Mountain) A 5-minute walk from St. Paul's Church, Römerberg is Frankfurt's historic heart, featuring picturesque half-timbered houses and the stunning Römer, a complex of medieval buildings that served as Frankfurt's city hall for over 600 years. Wander through this charming square and take in the atmosphere of old Frankfurt. Address: Römerberg, 60311 Frankfurt am Main

5:00 PM - Frankfurt Cathedral (Kaiserdom) Just a short walk from Römerberg, Frankfurt Cathedral, also known as Kaiserdom, is an impressive Gothic church that has played a significant role in German history. Although not a cathedral in the strictest sense (it has never been the seat of a bishop), it earned its nickname due to its importance during the Holy Roman Empire. Ten emperors were crowned within its walls between the 14th and 18th centuries. Take some time to explore the cathedral's stunning interior, including the Emperor's Hall (Kaisersaal) and the museum. Address: Domplatz 1, 60311 Frankfurt am Main Website: https://www.dom-frankfurt.de/en/

6:30 PM - Dinner at Zum Storch am Dom Located near the Frankfurt Cathedral, Zum Storch am Dom is a cozy, traditional restaurant offering delicious German and regional Hessian dishes. Try their hearty Rinderroulade (beef roulade) or Frankfurter Rippchen (smoked pork chops) to cap off your day exploring Frankfurt's historic sites. Address: Weckmarkt 13, 60311 Frankfurt am Main Website: https://www.zum-storch-am-dom.de/ Price Range: €15-€30

Day 2:

9:00 AM - Breakfast at Wacker's Kaffee Begin your second day with breakfast at Wacker's Kaffee, a family-owned café that has been serving delicious coffee and pastries in Frankfurt since 1914. Enjoy a variety of breakfast options in this cozy, historic café. Address: Kornmarkt 9, 60311 Frankfurt am Main Website: https://www.wackers-kaffee.de/ Price Range: €5-€15

10:00 AM - Goethe House and Goethe Museum Just a 5-minute walk from Wacker's Kaffee, the Goethe House is the birthplace of Germany's most famous writer, Johann Wolfgang von Goethe. This meticulously restored 18th-century home provides a fascinating insight into Goethe's life and times. After exploring the house, visit the adjacent Goethe Museum to learn more about the writer's work and legacy. Address: Großer Hirschgraben 23-25, 60311 Frankfurt am Main Website: https://www.goethehaus-frankfurt.de/goethehaus Admission: €7 for adults, €3 for students, free for children under 6

12:00 PM - Lunch at Café Hauptwache A 10-minute walk from the Goethe House, Café Hauptwache is located in the heart of Frankfurt and offers a variety of lunch options, from sandwiches and salads to traditional German dishes. Enjoy your meal in this historic 18th-century building. Address: An der Hauptwache 15, 60313 Frankfurt am Main Website: http://www.cafehauptwache.de/ Price Range: €10-€25

1:30 PM - Jewish Museum (Jüdisches Museum) After lunch, take a 15-minute walk to the Jewish Museum, which chronicles the rich history and culture of Frankfurt's Jewish community, dating back to the Middle Ages. The museum is housed in two historic buildings: the Rothschild Palais and the adjacent Judengasse Museum. Explore the thought-provoking exhibits and learn about the lives of Jewish people in Frankfurt throughout the centuries. Address: Untermainkai 14-15, 60311 Frankfurt am Main Website: https://www.juedischesmuseum.de/en/ Admission: €5 for adults, €2.50 for students, free for children under 6

3:30 PM - Kleinmarkthalle (Little Market Hall) From the Jewish Museum, walk for about 10 minutes to the Kleinmarkthalle, a bustling indoor market hall that has been a fixture of Frankfurt's culinary scene since 1954. With over 60 vendors selling fresh produce, meats, cheeses, and other local specialties, it's the perfect place to experience the flavors of the region. Sample traditional treats such as sausages, pretzels, and pastries, or pick up souvenirs like local honey or Frankfurt's famous green sauce (Grüne Soße). Address: Hasengasse 5-7, 60311 Frankfurt am Main Website: https://www.kleinmarkthalle.de/en/ Price Range: €3-€20

5:00 PM - Museum of Modern Art (MMK) Round off your historic walking tour with a visit to the Museum of Modern Art, located just a 5-minute walk from Kleinmarkthalle. Housed in a striking triangular building designed by architect Hans Hollein, the museum showcases an impressive collection of modern and contemporary art, including works by renowned artists such as Roy Lichtenstein, Gerhard Richter, and Andy Warhol. Address: Domstraße 10, 60311 Frankfurt am Main Website: https://mmk-frankfurt.de/en/home/

Admission: €12 for adults, €6 for students, free for children under 18

7:00 PM - Dinner at Margarete Cap off your two-day journey through Frankfurt's history with dinner at Margarete, a modern restaurant that combines traditional German cuisine with contemporary culinary influences. Enjoy their creative dishes made from locally sourced ingredients in a stylish, relaxed atmosphere. Address: Braubachstraße 18-22, 60311 Frankfurt am Main Website: https://www.margarete.restaurant/en/ Price Range: €15-€35

Throughout this two-day walking tour, you'll experience the rich history and cultural heritage of Frankfurt, from medieval fortifications and historic churches to the birthplace of Germany's most famous writer. As you explore the city on foot, take the time to appreciate the unique blend of old and new that makes Frankfurt such a captivating destination.

Embrace your journey through time as you uncover the historic treasures of Frankfurt and immerse yourself in the fascinating stories that have shaped this vibrant city.

Culinary Delights Itinerary: A Taste of Frankfurt's Food Scene

Day 1:

9:00 AM - Breakfast at Café Laumer Begin your culinary adventure with breakfast at Café Laumer, a charming traditional German café known for its pastries, bread, and coffee. Choose from a variety of breakfast options, including classic German fare and international dishes. Address: Bockenheimer Landstraße 67, 60325 Frankfurt am Main Website: https://www.cafe-laumer.de/en/ Price Range: €5-€15

10:30 AM - Kleinmarkthalle (Little Market Hall) After breakfast, take a 15-minute walk or the U-Bahn (U6 or U7) to Hauptwache station, followed by a short stroll to the Kleinmarkthalle. This bustling indoor market has been a cornerstone of Frankfurt's culinary scene since 1954. Explore the market's 60+ vendors offering fresh produce, meats, cheeses, and other regional specialties. Sample traditional treats like sausages, pretzels, and pastries, or pick up souvenirs such as local honey or Frankfurt's famous green sauce (Grüne Soße). Address: Hasengasse 5-7, 60311 Frankfurt am Main Website: https://www.kleinmarkthalle.de/en/ Price Range: €3-€20

1:00 PM - Lunch at Apfelweinwirtschaft Adolf Wagner Take a 20-minute walk or tram ride (lines 15 or 16) across the river to Sachsenhausen, a neighborhood known for its traditional apple wine taverns. Enjoy lunch at Apfelweinwirtschaft Adolf Wagner, where you can try classic Frankfurt dishes such as Handkäs mit Musik (marinated cheese with onions) or Frankfurter Rippchen (smoked pork chops) accompanied by a glass of the famous apple wine. Address: Schweizer Str. 71, 60594 Frankfurt am Main Website: http://www.adolf-wagner.de/ Price Range: €10-€25

3:00 PM - Ebbelwoi Express (Apple Wine Express) Discover Frankfurt from a different perspective aboard the Ebbelwoi Express, a historic tram that takes you on a leisurely tour of the city while you enjoy a glass of apple wine and pretzels. The 1-hour journey departs from the Frankfurt Zoo and takes you through the city's most iconic sights. Address: Zoo Frankfurt, Alfred-Brehm-Platz 16, 60316 Frankfurt am Main Website: https://www.ebbelwei-express.de/en/ Admission: €8 for adults, €3.50 for children (ages 6-14), including a glass of apple wine or a soft drink

5:00 PM - Chocolate Tasting at Bitter & Zart Chocolaterie Head back to the city center and indulge your sweet tooth with a chocolate tasting at Bitter & Zart Chocolaterie, a charming shop specializing in handcrafted chocolates, truffles, and other confections. Enjoy the delightful atmosphere and sample their exquisite creations. Address: Braubachstraße 14, 60311 Frankfurt am Main Website: https://www.bitterundzart.de/ Price Range: €3-€20

7:30 PM - Dinner at Restaurant Français Experience fine dining at Restaurant Français, located in the prestigious Steigenberger Frankfurter Hof hotel. This Michelin-starred restaurant offers an elegant setting and a seasonal menu featuring modern French cuisine with a German twist, using only the finest ingredients. Address: Am Kaiserplatz, 60311 Frankfurt am Main

Website: https://www.steigenberger.com/en/hotels/all-hotels/germany/frankfurt/steigenberger-frankfurter-hof/restaurants-bars Price Range: €45-€120

Day 2:

9:00 AM - Breakfast at Wacker's Kaffee Start your second day with breakfast at Wacker's Kaffee, a family-owned café that has been serving delicious coffee and pastries in Frankfurt since 1914. Enjoy a variety of breakfast options in this cozy, historic café. Address: Kornmarkt 9, 60311 Frankfurt am Main Website: https://www.wackers-kaffee.de/ Price Range: €5-€15

10:30 AM - German Film Museum Café After breakfast, take a 20-minute walk or tram ride (lines 14 or 18) to the German Film Museum Café, located along the Museum Embankment. This unique café offers not only coffee and cakes, but also a variety of film-related souvenirs and a small exhibition on German cinema. Enjoy a mid-morning snack while learning about the history of film in Germany. Address: Schaumainkai 41, 60596 Frankfurt am Main Website: https://www.deutsches-filminstitut.de/en/filmmuseum/ Price Range: €3-€10

12:30 PM - Lunch at Im Herzen Afrikas For lunch, try something different and head to Im Herzen Afrikas, an African restaurant offering a unique dining experience. Enjoy traditional dishes from Ethiopia and Eritrea, served in a cozy, authentic atmosphere. Make sure to try their Injera, a sourdough flatbread that accompanies most dishes. Address: Gutleutstraße 13, 60329 Frankfurt am Main Website: https://www.im-herzen-afrikas.com/ Price Range: €10-€25

3:00 PM - Café Siesmayer in Palmengarten After lunch, take a 20-minute walk or the U-Bahn (U4 or U5) to Bockenheimer Warte station, followed by a short stroll to Café Siesmayer, located within the picturesque Palmengarten. Enjoy a coffee and a slice of cake while admiring the beautiful botanical garden surroundings. Address: Siesmayerstraße 61, 60323 Frankfurt am Main Website: https://www.cafe-siesmayer.de/en/ Price Range: €3-€10

5:00 PM - Apfelwein Solzer Experience more of Frankfurt's traditional food scene with a visit to Apfelwein Solzer, a family-run apple wine tavern in the Bornheim neighborhood. Sample their apple wine varieties and try regional specialties like Grüne Soße (green sauce) or Hessian potato pancakes. Address: Berger Str. 260, 60385 Frankfurt am Main Website: https://www.apfelwein-solzer.de/en/ Price Range: €10-€25

7:30 PM - Dinner at The Ivory Club For your final dinner, treat yourself to a gourmet experience at The Ivory Club, an upscale restaurant offering a fusion of Asian and European flavors. The elegant atmosphere and beautifully presented dishes create a memorable dining experience. Address: Taubenstraße 1, 60313 Frankfurt am Main Website: https://www.ivory-club.de/en/ Price Range: €25-€65

This two-day itinerary showcases the diverse culinary delights of Frankfurt's food scene. You'll sample traditional Hessian dishes, indulge in gourmet experiences, and taste the flavors of Africa and Asia.

Green Frankfurt Itinerary: Exploring Parks and Nature

Title: Green Frankfurt: Exploring Parks and Nature

Day 1:

9:00 AM - Breakfast at Café Tasso Start your day with breakfast at Café T Tasso, a charming café serving a variety of breakfast options, including organic and vegetarian dishes. Enjoy your meal in the cozy atmosphere or sit outside in the picturesque courtyard. Address: An der Welle 3, 60322 Frankfurt am Main Website: https://www.cafe-tasso.de/ Price Range: €5-€15

10:30 AM - Palmengarten After breakfast, take a 20-minute walk or the U-B Bahn (U6 or U7) to Westturmark station, followed by a short stroll to Palmellschaft Palm Garden, a large botanical garden established in 1868 that features plants from all around the world. Explore the various greenhouses and themed gardens, and take a leisurely stroll around the picturesque pond. Address: Siesmayerstraße 61, 60323 Frankfurt am Main Website: https://www.palmengarten.de/en/ Ad Admission: €7 for adults, €2 for children (ages 6-14)

1:00 PM - Lunch at Brentano Café & Bistro in Brentano Park Make your way to Brentano Park, a 20-minute walk or a short bus ride (line 32) from the Palm Garden. Enjoy lunch at Brentano Café & Bistro, which offers a selection of sandwiches, salads, and other light fare in a charming setting overlooking the park. Address: Rottweiler Straße 32, 60322 Frankfurt am Main Price Range: €5-€15

2:30 PM - Nordsch Park After lunch, explore Nrs Nord Park, a vast green space that was once the site of the Bundesgartenschau (National Garden Show) in 1985. The park features numerous walking paths, a rose garden, a picturesque pond, and a variety of public art installations. There is also a playground for children and a small café for refreshments. Address: Ginnheimer Landstraße 5-13, 60487 Frankfurt am Main

5:00 PM - Grüneburger Green ug Park (Grüngü rt belt Park) Make your way to Grüngü Gü belt Park, a 30-minute walk or a 15-minute tram ride (line 16) from N Nord Park. This large green space is part of Frankfurt's "green belt belt," a network of parks and green spaces that enccircle the city. St Explore the park's walking paths, sports facilities, and playgrounds, or take a relaxing boat ride on the picturesque pond. Address: Gün G straße 2, 60318 Frankfurt am Main

7:00 PM - Dinner at Zur Sonne End your day with a traditional German dinner at Zur Sonne, a cozy restaurant located near Grüngelbelt Park. Enjoy a variety of German and Hessian dishes, such as schnitzel or Frank Frankfurter Rippchen, in a warm and welcoming atmosphere. Address: Berger Str. 312, 60385 Frankfurt am Main Website: http://www.zursonne-fr.com/ Price Range: €10-€25

Day 2:

9:00 AM - Breakfast at Café Karin Start your second day with breakfast at Café Karin, a popular local café offering a variety of breakfast options, including homemade pastries and fresh bread. Enjoy the cozy atmosphere and friendly service. Address: Großer Hirschgraben 28, 60311 Frankfurt am Main Website: http://www.cafekarin.de/ Price Range: €5-€15

10:30 AM - Frankfurt City Forest (Stadtwald) After breakfast, head to the Frankfurt City Forest, a 20-minute drive or a 30-minute tram ride (line 17) from Café Karin. The Stadtwald is Germany's largest inner-city forest, offering miles of walking and biking trails, picturesque ponds, and playgrounds. Enjoy a morning walk or bike ride in this serene natural setting. Address: 60528 Frankfurt am Main

1:00 PM - Lunch at Restaurant Oberschweinstiege Located in the heart of the Frankfurt City Forest, Restaurant Oberschweinstiege offers a tranquil setting for a leisurely lunch. Enjoy a selection of German and international dishes, such as schnitzel or seasonal salads, in the rustic dining room or on the outdoor terrace. Address: Oberschweinstiege 16, 60598 Frankfurt am Main Website: https://www.restaurant-oberschweinstiege.de/ Price Range: €10-€25

2:30 PM - Visit the Goethe Tower (Goetheturm) After lunch, make your way to the Goethe Tower, a 43-meter-tall wooden observation tower located within the Frankfurt City Forest. Climb the 196 steps to the top for panoramic views of the city skyline and the surrounding forest. Address: Sachsenhauser Landwehrweg 1, 60599 Frankfurt am Main Admission: Free

4:00 PM - Lohrberg Park (Lohrberg) Next, head to Lohrberg Park, a 20-minute drive or a 30-minute tram ride (line 14) from the Goethe Tower. This park is located on a hill and offers sweeping views of Frankfurt's skyline. Stroll through the terraced gardens, relax in the orchard, or visit the vineyard, where you can sample locally produced wine. Address: Auf dem Lohr 9, 60389 Frankfurt am Main

6:30 PM - Dinner at Zum Gemalten Haus End your day with dinner at Zum Gemalten Haus, a traditional apple wine tavern located in the Sachsenhausen district. Enjoy classic Frankfurt dishes such as Grüne Soße or Handkäs mit Musik, accompanied by a glass of the famous apple wine. Address: Schweizer Str. 67, 60594 Frankfurt am Main Website: https://www.zumgemaltenhaus.de/ Price Range: €10-€25

This two-day itinerary takes you on a journey through Frankfurt's green spaces, from botanical gardens and city parks to the vast Frankfurt City Forest. Enjoy the natural beauty of the city and discover hidden gems that offer a peaceful respite from the urban bustle.

Frankfurt After Dark Itinerary: Nightlife and Entertainment

Day 1:

7:00 PM - Dinner at Druckwasserwerk Begin your evening with dinner at Druckwasserwerk, a restaurant housed in a former industrial building, offering a unique atmosphere and a menu featuring German and international cuisine. The restaurant's riverside location offers beautiful views of the Main River. Address: Rotfeder-Ring 16, 60327 Frankfurt am Main Website: https://www.druckwasserwerk-frankfurt.de/ Price Range: €15-€35

9:00 PM - Sunset Drinks at Main Tower Observation Deck Head to the Main Tower, a 56-story skyscraper, and take the elevator to the observation deck on the 54th floor. Enjoy panoramic views of Frankfurt's skyline while sipping a cocktail or a glass of wine at the bar. The observation deck is open until 11:00 PM on Fridays and Saturdays. Address: Neue Mainzer Straße 52-58, 60311 Frankfurt am Main Website: https://www.maintower.de/en/ Admission: €9.50 for adults, €5.50 for children (ages 6-12)

10:30 PM - Gibson Club Experience Frankfurt's vibrant nightlife scene at Gibson Club, a popular live music venue and nightclub located on the famous Zeil shopping street. The club features an eclectic mix of musical genres, including jazz, rock, hip-hop, and electronic music. Check their website for the event schedule and ticket prices. Address: Zeil 85-93, 60313 Frankfurt am Main Website: https://www.gibson-club.de/ Price Range: €10-€20 for entry, plus drink prices

1:00 AM - Late Night Snack at Best Worscht in Town Satisfy your late-night cravings at Best Worscht in Town, a legendary Frankfurt fast-food joint specializing in currywurst, a German street food classic. Choose your preferred spice level and enjoy the delicious combination of sausage, curry sauce, and crispy fries. Address:

Schäfergasse 29, 60313 Frankfurt am Main Website: https://www.bestworschtintown.de/ Price Range: €4-€10

Day 2:

7:00 PM - Dinner at Margarete Start your evening with dinner at Margarete, a modern restaurant offering a fusion of German and international cuisine made from locally sourced ingredients. The stylish atmosphere and central location make it an ideal spot for dinner before a night out. Address: Braubachstraße 18-22, 60311 Frankfurt am Main Website: https://www.margarete-restaurant.de/en/ Price Range: €15-€35

9:00 PM - Jazz at Jazzkeller Experience live jazz music at Jazzkeller, Frankfurt's oldest and most iconic jazz club, which has been hosting legendary jazz musicians since 1952. Check their website for the event schedule and ticket prices, and enjoy a night of exceptional music in this intimate and historic venue. Address: Kleine Bockenheimer Str. 18a, 60313 Frankfurt am Main Website: https://www.jazzkeller.com/ Price Range: €10-€25 for entry, plus drink prices

11:30 PM - Cocktails at The Kinly Bar Head to The Kinly Bar, an atmospheric speakeasy-style cocktail bar located in Frankfurt's Bahnhofsviertel district. The expert mixologists create unique and innovative cocktails using high-quality ingredients, ensuring a memorable experience. Address: Elbestraße 31, 60329 Frankfurt am Main

Website: https://www.thekinlybar.com/ Price Range: €10-€15 for cocktails

1:00 AM - Dance at Club Travolta Keep the party going at Club Travolta, a trendy nightclub in the heart of Frankfurt. The club features two floors with different music styles, ranging from hip-hop and R&B to house and electronic beats. Dance the night away in this lively and stylish venue. Address: Querstraße 3-7, 60329

Frankfurt am Main Website: https://www.club-travolta.de/ Price Range: €10-€15 for entry, plus drink prices

3:00 AM - Late-Night Bite at Imbiss bei Schorsch Cap off your night with a visit to Imbiss bei Schorsch, a popular late-night food spot known for its delicious grilled sausages and other German fast-food options. Soak up the night's festivities with a tasty snack before heading back to your accommodation. Address: Allerheiligenstraße 20, 60313 Frankfurt am Main Price Range: €3-€10

This two-day itinerary takes you on a journey through Frankfurt's vibrant nightlife and entertainment scene. From live music venues and trendy cocktail bars to lively nightclubs and late-night food joints, there's something for everyone to enjoy after the sun goes down in Frankfurt.

Modern Marvels Itinerary: Skyscrapers and Architectural Wonders

Day 1:

10:00 AM - Breakfast at Wacker's Kaffee Start your day with breakfast at Wacker's Kaffee, a traditional Frankfurt café known for its excellent coffee and delicious pastries. Fuel up for a day of exploring the city's modern architecture. Address: Kornmarkt 9, 60311 Frankfurt am Main Website: https://www.wackers-kaffee.com/ Price Range: €5-€15

11:00 AM - Main Tower Begin your architectural tour with a visit to the Main Tower, a 56-story skyscraper that offers panoramic views of the city from its observation deck on the 54th floor. Designed by architect Helmut Jahn, the building is a shining example of modern architecture in Frankfurt. Address: Neue Mainzer Straße 52-58,

60311 Frankfurt am Main Website: https://www.maintower.de/en/
Admission: €9.50 for adults, €5.50 for children (ages 6-12)

12:30 PM - Lunch at The Squaire Head to The Squaire, a massive office and hotel complex located near Frankfurt Airport. The building's unique design, with its wave-like shape and striking glass façade, makes it a must-see for architecture enthusiasts. Enjoy lunch at one of the many restaurants and cafés within the complex. Address: The Squaire, 60549 Frankfurt am Main Price Range: €10-€25

2:00 PM - European Central Bank (ECB) After lunch, visit the European Central Bank, the institution responsible for monetary policy in the Eurozone. The ECB's headquarters is a striking example of modern architecture, featuring a twisted double-tower design connected by a glass atrium. Note that the interior of the building is not open to the public, but the exterior is worth admiring. Address: Sonnemannstraße 20, 60314 Frankfurt am Main Website: https://www.ecb.europa.eu/

3:30 PM - Westhafen Tower Continue your architectural tour with a visit to Westhafen Tower, a 30-story skyscraper located in Frankfurt's Westhafen district. The building's unique glass façade, designed to resemble the ripples of water, has earned it the nickname "The Crown." Address: Westhafenplatz 1, 60327 Frankfurt am Main

5:00 PM - Skyline Plaza End your day with a visit to Skyline Plaza, a shopping center and entertainment complex with a unique design that features a large, undulating glass roof. Browse the many shops, enjoy dinner at one of the numerous restaurants, or relax in the spa and wellness area. Address: Europa-Allee 6, 60327 Frankfurt am Main Website: https://www.skylineplaza.de/en/ Price Range: Varies depending on activities and restaurants

Day 2:

10:00 AM - Breakfast at Café Crumble Start your second day with breakfast at Café Crumble, a cozy café that offers a variety of delicious breakfast options, including homemade pastries and fresh bread. Address: Kiesstraße 41, 60486 Frankfurt am Main Website: https://www.cafe-crumble.de/ Price Range: €5-€15

11:00 AM - Taunus Tower and OpernTurm Begin your day with a visit to the Taunus Tower and OpernTurm, two modern skyscrapers located in the heart of Frankfurt's financial district. The Taunus Tower features a minimalist design and a striking glass façade, while the OpernTurm combines contemporary architecture with a preserved historic façade at its base. Address: Taunusanlage 8, 60329 Frankfurt am Main (Taunus Tower); Bockenheimer Landstraße 2-4, 60306 Frankfurt am Main (OpernTurm)

12:30 PM - Lunch at Alex Frankfurt Skyline Plaza Head back to Skyline Plaza and have lunch at Alex, a trendy restaurant offering a diverse menu with a mix of German and international dishes, as well as a spectacular view of Frankfurt's skyline from its rooftop terrace. Address: Europa-Allee 6, 60327 Frankfurt am Main Website: https://www.dein-alex.de/frankfurt-skyline-plaza Price Range: €10-€25

2:00 PM - MyZeil Shopping Center Visit the MyZeil Shopping Center, a modern architectural wonder designed by architect Massimiliano Fuksas. Its most striking feature is the enormous glass vortex that extends from the roof to the ground level. Explore the various shops and enjoy the unique architecture. Address: Zeil 106, 60313 Frankfurt am Main Website: https://www.myzeil.de/ Price Range: Varies depending on shopping preferences

4:00 PM - PalaisQuartier Continue your architectural tour at PalaisQuartier, a mixed-use development that combines historic buildings with modern architecture. The complex includes the reconstructed Palais Thurn und Taxis, the striking Nextower, and the luxurious Jumeirah Frankfurt hotel. Address: Thurn-und-Taxis-

Platz 6, 60313 Frankfurt am Main Website: https://www.palais-frankfurt.de/en

6:00 PM - Dinner at VaiVai Frankfurt Conclude your day with dinner at VaiVai Frankfurt, a modern Italian restaurant located in the heart of the city. The restaurant's industrial-chic design and diverse menu make it a fitting end to your exploration of Frankfurt's modern architecture. Address: Grüneburgweg 16, 60322 Frankfurt am Main Website: https://vaivai.de/ Price Range: €15-€35

This two-day itinerary showcases the best of Frankfurt's modern architecture, from towering skyscrapers and innovative designs to impressive shopping centers and urban developments. Immerse yourself in the city's contemporary side and marvel at the architectural wonders that define Frankfurt's skyline.

Family Fun in Frankfurt: Activities for All Ages

Day 1:

9:00 AM - Breakfast at Café Laumer Start your day with breakfast at Café Laumer, a charming café that offers a variety of delicious breakfast options, including pastries, bread, and coffee. It's the perfect spot to fuel up for a day of family fun in Frankfurt. Address: Bockenheimer Landstraße 67, 60325 Frankfurt am Main Website: https://www.cafe-laumer.de/ Price Range: €5-€15

10:00 AM - Palmengarten Begin your day with a visit to Palmengarten, Frankfurt's beautiful botanical garden. With its extensive collection of plants and flowers from around the world, Palmengarten is a great place for children to explore and learn about different ecosystems. There are also several playgrounds and interactive exhibits designed for kids. Address: Siesmayerstraße 61,

60323 Frankfurt am Main Website:
https://www.palmengarten.de/en/ Admission: €7 for adults, €2 for children (ages 6-13)

1:00 PM - Lunch at Wilma Wunder Enjoy a family-friendly lunch at Wilma Wunder, a restaurant offering a mix of German and international dishes made from fresh, locally sourced ingredients. The restaurant has a special kids' menu, as well as coloring sheets and crayons to keep little ones entertained. Address: An der Hauptwache 15, 60313 Frankfurt am Main Website: https://wilma-wunder.de/en/ Price Range: €10-€25

2:30 PM - Senckenberg Natural History Museum Spend the afternoon exploring the Senckenberg Natural History Museum, one of the largest natural history museums in Germany. The museum offers a fascinating collection of exhibits on dinosaurs, fossils, and other natural wonders, making it an ideal destination for families with curious kids. Address: Senckenberganlage 25, 60325 Frankfurt am Main Website: https://www.senckenberg.de/en/ Admission: €10 for adults, €5 for children (ages 6-15)

5:00 PM - Ebbelwei Express Climb aboard the Ebbelwei Express, a historic tram that takes visitors on a guided tour of Frankfurt's city center while providing a fun introduction to the city's history and culture. The tram offers a relaxed atmosphere, with traditional Frankfurt music and complimentary apple juice for kids. Address: Start at Frankfurt Zoo, Bernhard-Grzimek-Allee 1, 60316 Frankfurt am Main Website: https://www.ebbelwei-express.de/en/ Ticket Price: €8 for adults, €3.50 for children (ages 6-14)

7:00 PM - Dinner at Apfelwein Wagner End your day with a traditional Frankfurt dinner at Apfelwein Wagner, a historic tavern serving classic German dishes like schnitzel and sausages, as well as a selection of non-alcoholic beverages for the kids. Address: Schweizer Str. 71, 60594 Frankfurt am Main Website: http://www.apfelwein-wagner.com/ Price Range: €10-€25

Day 2:

9:00 AM - Breakfast at Café & Bar Celona Start your second day with breakfast at Café & Bar Celona, a modern café offering a variety of breakfast options, including sandwiches, pastries, and fresh juices. Address: Holzgraben 31, 60313 Frankfurt am Main Website: https://www.cafe-bar-celona.de/en/ Price Range: €5-€15

10:00 AM - Frankfurt Zoo Begin your day with a visit to Frankfurt Zoo, home to over 4,500 animals representing more than 500 species. With its diverse range of exhibits, the zoo offers an engaging and educational experience for the whole family. Don't miss the Grzimek House, a unique indoor exhibit featuring nocturnal animals and their natural habitats. Address: Bernhard-Grzimek-Allee 1, 60316 Frankfurt am Main Website: https://www.zoo-frankfurt.de/en/ Admission: €12 for adults, €6 for children (ages 6-15)

1:00 PM - Lunch at Freitagsküche Head to Freitagsküche for a family-friendly lunch in a relaxed atmosphere. This popular restaurant offers a selection of German and international dishes prepared with fresh, local ingredients. Address: Münchener Str. 20, 60329 Frankfurt am Main Website: http://freitagskueche.de/ Price Range: €10-€25

2:30 PM - Experimenta Science Center Spend the afternoon at Experimenta Science Center, an interactive museum designed to inspire curiosity and learning about science, technology, engineering, and mathematics (STEM). With hands-on exhibits and engaging workshops, Experimenta is a great destination for families with kids of all ages. Address: Hafenpark Quartier, Deutschherrnufer 41, 60594 Frankfurt am Main Website: https://www.experimenta.science/en/ Admission: €16 for adults, €12 for children (ages 4-17)

5:00 PM - Mainu Mall Take a break from sightseeing and head to the Main-Taunus-Zentrum, a large shopping center located just outside of Frankfurt. The mall offers a wide range of shops, restaurants, and entertainment options, including a cinema and a kids' play area. Address: Main-Taunus-Zentrum 1, 65843 Sulzbach (Taunus) Website: https://www.main-taunus-zentrum.de/en/ Price Range: Varies depending on shopping preferences and activities

7:00 PM - Dinner at L'Osteria Frankfurt Ostend End your day with a family dinner at L'Osteria Frankfurt Ostend, a lively Italian restaurant offering a variety of delicious pasta dishes, pizzas, and salads. The restaurant has a kids' menu and a welcoming atmosphere, making it a great option for families. Address: Hanauer Landstraße 127, 60314 Frankfurt am Main Website: https://losteria.de/en/ Price Range: €10-€25

This two-day itinerary is packed with family-friendly activities and attractions in Frankfurt, providing fun and entertainment for all ages. From exploring botanical gardens and natural history museums to enjoying interactive science exhibits and visiting the city's zoo, your family will create lasting memories during your time in Frankfurt.

Frankfurt Map of all the spots in the Itineraries

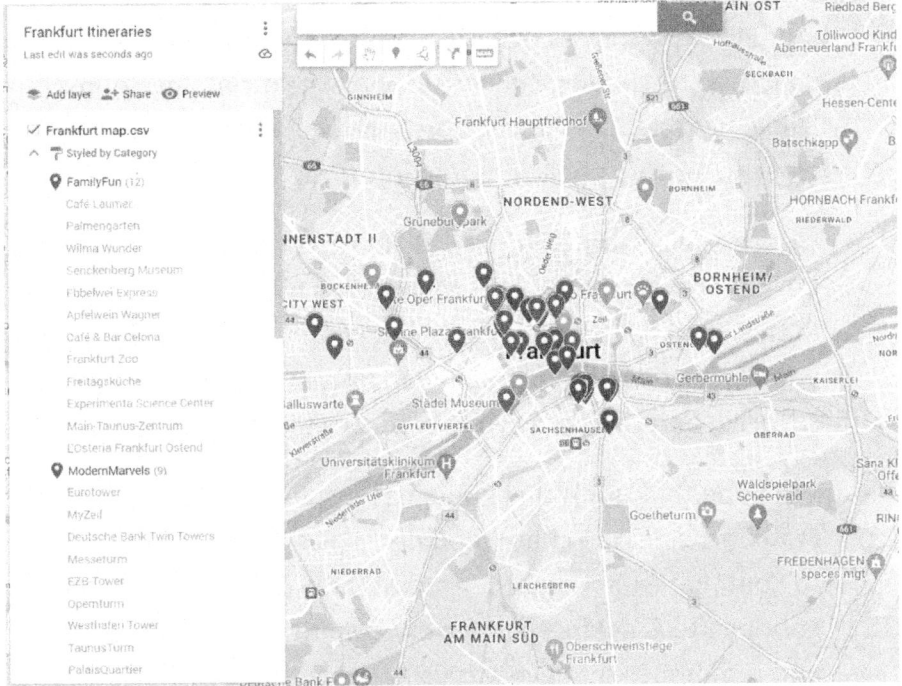

You can get the online google maps of all the spots in the itineraries above at bit.ly/frankfurtitineraries

Thank you

As you wrap up your unforgettable journey through Frankfurt, it's time to reflect on the memories you've created while exploring this vibrant city. From its rich history, architectural marvels, and green spaces to its thriving culinary scene, world-class museums, and lively nightlife, Frankfurt offers a diverse array of experiences that cater to visitors of all ages and interests.

Our carefully curated itineraries have guided you through the very best of Frankfurt, ensuring that you've made the most of your time in this bustling metropolis. As you return home, you'll carry with you the stories of the people you've met, the flavors you've savored, and the sights you've encountered along the way.

We hope that our travel guide has inspired you to delve deeper into Frankfurt's unique charm and perhaps even sparked your curiosity to continue exploring other remarkable destinations. As you say goodbye to Frankfurt, let the city's spirit continue to inspire you, and remember that every journey is an opportunity to discover new perspectives and create lasting memories. Safe travels, and until next time, auf Wiedersehen!

Copyright Notice

Guidora Frankfurt in 3 Days Travel Guide ©

Disclaimer

The publishers have checked the information in this travel guide but its accuracy is not warranted or guaranteed. Frankfurt visitors are advised that opening times should always be checked before making a journey.

Tracing Copyright Owners

Every effort has been made to trace the copyright holders of referred material. Where these efforts have not been successful, copyright owners are invited to contact the editor (Guidora) so that their copyright can be acknowledged and/or the material removed from the publication.

Creative Commons Content

We are most grateful to publishers of Creative Commons material, including images. Our policies concerning this material are (1) to credit the copyright owner, and provide a link where possible (2) to remove Creative Commons material, at once, if the copyright owner so requests - for example if the owner changes the licensing of an image.

We will also keep our interpretation of the Creative Commons Non-Commercial license under review. Along with, we believe, most web publishers, our current view is that acceptance of the 'Non-Commercial' condition means (1) we must not sell the image or any publication containing the image (2) we may however use an image as an illustration for some information which is not being sold or offered for sale.

Note to other copyright owners

We are grateful to those copyright owners who have given permission for their material to be used. Some of the material in the comes from secondary and tertiary sources. In every case we have tried to locate the original author or photographer and make the appropriate acknowledgement. In some cases the sources have proved obscure and we have been unable to track them down. In these cases, we would like to hear from the copyright owners and will be pleased to acknowledge them in future editions or remove the material.

Printed in Great Britain
by Amazon

28247368R00056